DATE DUE

			PRINTED IN U.S.A.

A Taste of Périgord

HELEN RAIMES

Illustrations by Jenny Ibrahim

ROBERT HALE · LONDON

© *Helen Raimes 1991*
First published in Great Britain 1991

ISBN 0 7090 4389 9

Robert Hale Limited
Clerkenwell House
Clerkenwell Green
London EC1R 0HT

The right of Helen Raimes to be identified as
author of this work has been asserted by her
in accordance with the Copyright, Designs and
Patents Act 1988.

Illustrations by Jenny Ibrahim.
Map of Périgord by Amanda Tempest-Radford.

Photoset in North Wales by
Derek Doyle & Associates, Mold, Clwyd.
Printed in Great Britain by
St Edmundsbury Press Ltd, Bury St Edmunds, Suffolk.
and bound by WBC Bookbinders Ltd, Bridgend, Glamorgan.

Contents

Dedication

The Périgord is a luscious land of plenty, a land where nature's bounty is appreciated to the full and where nothing is wasted, from the young dandelion shoots of February to the walnuts of November, from the tiny freshwater shrimp to the massive livers of the *gavés* geese. This book is an attempt to capture the taste of Périgord, and is dedicated to all my Périgordin friends who have so gladly shared their art and their enthusiasm with an outsider.

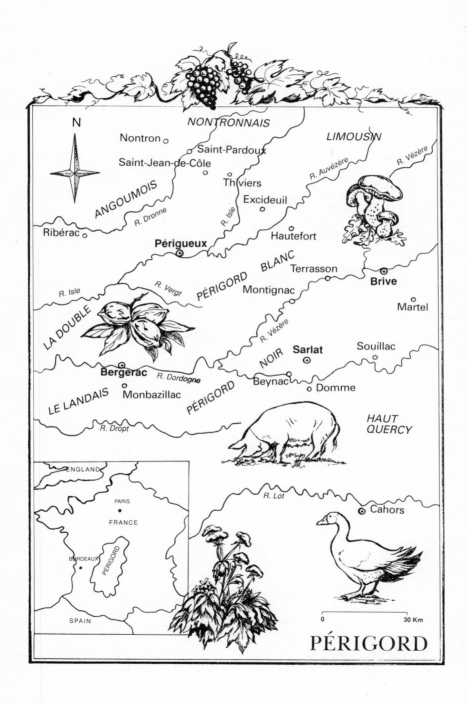

N

NONTRONNAIS

Nontron

Saint-Pardoux

Saint-Jean-de-Côle

LIMOUSIN

R. Vézère

R. Auvézère

Thiviers

Excideuil

ANGOUMOIS

R. Dronne

R. Isle

Ribérac

Périgueux

Hautefort

PÉRIGORD BLANC

Terrasson

Brive

R. Isle

R. Vergt

Montignac

Martel

LA DOUBLE

R. Vézère

NOIR

Sarlat

Souillac

Bergerac

R. Dordogne

Beynac

Domme

LE LANDAIS

Monbazillac

PÉRIGORD

HAUT
QUERCY

R. Dropt

ENGLAND

PARIS

FRANCE

R. Lot

Cahors

BORDEAUX

PÉRIGORD

SPAIN

0   30 Km

PÉRIGORD

Le Périgord

The Périgord lies between the Limousin and the valleys of Aquitaine, and is slightly less in area than the present département of the Dordogne. It is called after the Petrocorii, who lived there at the time of the Gauls. Five rivers enrich the land: the Dronne, the Isle, the Auvézère, the Vézère and the Dordogne, and it is these waters that give the area its striking diversity. The Périgord hasn't one face but a hundred faces, perhaps the most youthful along the Dronne and the Isle, the most blooming along the Dordogne and the Auvézère, and the most ancient along the valley of the low Vézère where prehistoric man hunted bison, rhinoceros and wild horse.

Many smaller watercourses, numerous rivulets, meander through the countryside, determining at the same time its seductive beauty and its human settlements. It was the five rivers and the myriad streams that caused the Romans to give the area the name of Aquitaine (*aqua*: water), while the Celtic word for water, '*onne*', forms many of the rivers' names: Garonne, Dronne, Lisonne, Beauronne, and so on. The Garonne, on which Bordeaux is built and which carried the Vikings and Romans inland to Périgord, is the greatest river of Aquitaine. Though both the Dordogne and the Isle are also navigable at their western reaches, neither can compete with the Garonne for commercial importance. Sometimes man and nature complement one another, sometimes man lets well alone. What 'improvement' could man make to a great river whose banks contain the ideal nourishment for some of the finest wines in the world? The soil is right, the climate is right, and there is no better way to transport wine than by water.

The river Dordogne is almost as long as, but less abundant than, the Garonne. Two little streams, the Dore and the Dogne, meet about a kilometre from their sources in the Puy de Sancy to form the main river, which has forged a valley more than a hundred kilometres long: perhaps the most fertile and picturesque valley in the whole of France. The Dordogne leaves Périgord to flow through the Bordeaux vineyards (*les vignobles bordelais*) forming, as it curves to meet the Garonne at the Bec d'Aubez, that strip of land famous for its white wines, Les Entre Deux Mers.

The Isle and the Vézère are both lesser rivers than the Dordogne. They rise in the plateaux of Limousin and run over the impermeable land to the north and north-east, which accounts for their frequent flooding in times of high rainfall and their reduction in summer. Neither of them have the clarity of waters born in the Périgord. Veins breaking out from the main streams pick up tiny particles of granite and rock which give the water a sombre, reddish tinge.

Despite tourism and the motorist, one cannot help but be moved by the Vézère. Its banks have been haunted by man for more than a thousand centuries. The fragile traces of our ancestors who hunted mammoths and carved statues from bones and stones touch the modern heart and mind, even at high season. The great enigma, Man's Evil, becomes ever more mysterious as one looks back from the twentieth century into the dark grottoes and half-lit cliff shelters of men who could go far underground to paint sensitive, elegant pictures of the creatures abounding in the woods and valleys around them. This place, the valley of the low Vézère, is the cradle of our race. There are other grottoes, other caves in Périgord – around Domme, the bastide town breathtakingly perched above the Dordogne itself, for instance, caves where centuries later the townspeople sheltered among bison and rhinoceros bones from the attacking Huguenots – but the shelters hollowed out of the limestone cliffs above the Vézère were the homes of our most distant ancestors. It is *here* that human intelligence woke to art and to diligence. One may become attached to the Périgord by its beauty, by its wonderful food, by its ancient buildings seemingly grown from the soil – but this is where we began. The earth along the banks of the low Vézère between La Madeleine and Les Eyzies bears the footprints that, step by step, link the generations. (There is no specific French connection there: the Périgord, lying almost entirely between the 1st and 2nd degrees longitude west, crossed at its widest point by the 15th degree latitude north and lying equidistant between the equator and the pole drew man and beast into its influences through the idyllic consequences of its geography.)

The Auvézère, as its name suggests, is a tributary of the Vézère and, though it also rises in the plateaux of the Limousin, it has a different character from the Vézère, an attractive domesticity one might say. It runs through farmlands in the Limousin before looping its way through the Périgord Noir to join up with the Isle. The domesticity of the river is emphasized by the continuing use of its water by the picturesque mills of St Mesmin and Pervendoux, and by the market gardens and walnut plantations which flourish along the alluvial soil of the valley.

It may be thought that I am making rather a lot of the waters of Périgord, but the two are indissolubly linked – and it is fitting that the story about the Dronne which follows should have come to me beside the waters of my village. The village is in the Périgord Noir, some 300 metres above sea-level, and is blessed with numerous springs which, even in recent summers of drought, have not failed us. The village 'lavoir', a specially constructed pool trapping the waters from a spring that rises a few feet from my walls, is not only still used for the washing – metered water keeps traditional methods alive – but is a favourite spot to pause and chat. The lavoir wall is seldom out of the sun, even in winter, and the old people come to sit on the warmed stone and hold their faces to the sun as they talk. I was sitting on the wall one evening, thinking about the Dronne, when I was joined by old Monsieur Fronsac. M. Fronsac is ninety and is another of the Périgord's rich springs: he has a phenomenal memory, which he attributes to a regular diet of garlic, and when I spoke to him of the Dronne he rested his chin on his hands crossed over the top of his stick and recited the following passage:

> The Dronne could say: 'In Limousin I was ugly, but in Périgord I am pretty. Up there, not far from here, I was trapped in a dark gorge and the shadows of my prison made my waters even darker. I ran through crystalline schists, with banks so close that often the wolf could straddle me at a bound. In summer the water caught in my locks has no power to turn my little mills, but soon I come to a deep, shady coombe and the waterfall of Chalard, near to St Pardoux. I run through the limestone and chalk of Périgord, and with no other help than this I am cleansed, fresh, beautiful, welcoming, open – no longer a gloomy torrent! Pure currents from deep springs flow in my bed and turn me into a delight.
> 'My sister, the Isle, whom I meet at Coutras, resembles me in many ways, but she is too Limousine when she comes into le Pays [the country] for these waters to give her the same gift of clarity that they give me'.

This passage throws an interesting light on the French methods of instructing the young mind. M. Fronsac learnt it from one of his daughter's school-books, printed either during the 39–45 war or just after. It also illustrates their profound ties with the region: 'le Pays' is Périgord. When a Périgordin says *'mon pays'* (*'moun pais'* in patois), he does not mean France.

The land mass of Périgord, geographically, is divided into two distinct parts on a line running approximately through Nontron, St Pardoux, Thiviers, Exideuil, Hautefort and Terrasson. The northern lands, impermeable rock and granite, form an advanced bastion of the Massif-Central, known as *'le grand noyau résistant de France'* (the great resistant core of France), while the central and southern lands are predominantly limestone and chalk, and these strata have been a wonderful source of water conservation: the rain filters through the limestone to a great depth to replenish Périgord's abundant springs.

Seen in relief, the Périgord gives the impression of a land in transition, a land falling gradually, gently, from the heights to the north and north-east towards the Gironde and the sea. Over 40% of its surface is forested and, though timber is both a principal industry and a domestic source of energy, scrupulous coppicing maintains a life-giving balance in the environment. In other respects the ecology will not surmount man's suicidal drift without strict controls. In 1989 almost no rain fell in Périgord and although, relative to other parts of the globe, there is water and purity in this environment, the time has come for even the Périgordins to heed the warnings. For the *moment*, there are mosses and lichens to be found in Périgord which have been killed by pollution elsewhere, and the spring that feeds our lavoir has been given a clean bill of health on analysis by our local doctors, who recommend that at least two litres of its waters should be drunk daily. (Though I haven't seen the doctors filling their buckets from the source, many of their patients follow the prescription.) With so much beauty around them it has been natural for Périgordins to take it for granted, but local pressure groups and local councils alike are now working to protect le Pays.

The essential image of the region is unlikely to change. Since the Second World War, farmers have been encouraged to modernize their methods and their equipment and to form co-operatives to further their interests. They have been encouraged to develop those crops for which the soil is particularly favourable, such as walnuts, truffles and fruit-trees. Recent years have shown a drift away from the farms. Farmers' daughters have either been educated off the land or have seen a city desk and painted nails as an easier option, thus creating a generation of celibate farmers, but there are signs of a shift in the wind. Architects are reporting that young people are restoring farms their parents neglected. There is the awareness of the ecology, of the environment, a new look at different qualities of life, hopeful signs of youth returning to the villages.

Before leaving me that evening on the lavoir wall to go to '*la soupe*', Grandpère Fronsac gave me another passage from his daughter's school-book:

If the savage is attached to his desert, the mountain-dweller to the arid rocks and the eskimo to the frozen wastes, with what tender pride must we cherish our smiling valleys and life-giving waters, our hills clothed with vines and oaks, the wide horizons of our plateaux, our countryside turn by turn gracious or wild, ennobled by the ancient traces of earliest man and those venerable ruins bequeathed to us by centuries of our history.

Ah, how often the sons of Périgord abandon their little country for the towns where they believe life will be easier and more amusing. And how many of these uprooted searchers after a mistaken mirage regret having left the parental roof, the native hills, the familiar lanes ... and the lost sweetness of evenings by the waters of Périgord.

The modern school-book may have changed in style, but the sentiment will still be there. Last year's bestseller in the region was a T-shirt inscribed *'Périgord, moun pais'*. There is a deep love of tradition and continuity under the modern façade. A man may leave his 'pays' to find work in Paris or Toulouse, but he buys a plot and builds on the earth of his origins, or he keeps tight hold of inherited property to finish his days where he began his days. When one of my visitors confessed that he had carried a little bag of English soil in his battledress pocket through World War II, even the great resistant heart of M. Tonneau was touched. Patriotism, specifically for the region, reaches its zenith here because the Périgordins *know* that their land has the best of everything France has to offer. There are all the maladies of an economy that puts the silicon chip before the *vrai pomme-de-terre*, but 'moun pais' is the string round the Périgordin parcel. This is the region where traditions are retained and nourished, where the sonorous patois may still be heard on the warmed stones of the lavoir walls, where a great resistant core of pride keeps the true flavour of Périgord alive.

The Roots of the Matter

INTRODUCTION

La Cuisine (cookery) in Périgord is, above all, the art of the women. This is an area where change comes slowly, particularly changes in attitude, and I am glad to say that I have forgotten which man said 'Cooking is patience, hence feminine'. The Rights of Man give man an equal right to patience, but apart from M. Tonneau, a man of extraordinary impatience who makes the pâté and cures the hams of the household, no other man in this commune interests himself in *La Cuisine Périgourdine* beyond enjoying or criticizing the delicacies set before him daily. There have been famous Périgordin chefs and *traiteurs* (caterers), such as Courtois and Villereynier, whose game and poultry terrines were renowned throughout the courts of Europe in the eighteenth century, André Noël, a sauce chef at the court of Frederick of Prussia, and the great Michelet whom Talleyrand took with him to the Congress of Vienna (perhaps in the hope of mellowing the mood of his adversaries), but these men are rarefied exceptions. The true test of a region's cookery rests not in the specialities on the table of the grand houses however, but on the everyday boards of the humble homes. Pâté de foie gras and game and poultry conserves (*les confits*) are synonymous with the Périgord, but the delicacy of such simple dishes as a *Tarte à Salfifis* or a *Poulet au Grain au Verjus* (Salsify Tart and Corn-fed Chicken with Verjuice), two matter-of-fact dishes for every day within the reach of the modest cook, must be the measure of Périgourdin quality. Whether by instinct mixed with inclination or perforce, the women here do seem to know how to enhance the simplest ingredients, how to transform mundane left-overs into mouthwatering masterpieces, how to blend and marry flavours with the subtlety and certainty of an artist mixing his colours.

It would seem that giving information and explanations is also an intrinsic Périgourdin quality, for none of my teachers has been too rushed or too impatient to demonstrate the simplest detail of a recipe or a method. The commune has taken an enthusiastic interest in my researches into their cuisine and customs, and the dedication of this book is no empty formality.

To give a list of what the Périgordin doesn't eat would not be appropriate to a book on their cookery, but I have chosen a calmer alternative to putting the reader through a vertiginous catalogue of what the Périgordin *does* eat. Igor Stravinsky stated that 'music and cookery are all one' and, yes, the recipe is the score (you miss a bar and it all falls apart), the utensils and the ingredients are the instruments and all comes together to create a work in which time has played its part. The servers of the dish are the musicians and he who directs them is the chef – appropriately, cooks frequently refer to their ovens as 'the piano'. I can hardly do better than take the beat from Stravinsky and my alternative to spanning several octaves of the Périgourdin diet will be to give the ground base for their cuisine.

THE GROUND BASE

La Cuisine Périgourdine is based on goose fat and walnut oil. These can be replaced by butter or pork fat, but it must be realized that the essential flavour of the dishes will be different from the original truly Périgourdin recipe. Goose fat has the advantage that it keeps a very long time – indeed, there are those who say that, like wine, it actually improves with age. Mme Tonneau, one of the commune's devout traditionalists, preserves both goose and pork fat in the old way, in 'toupines'. She told me recently that she is presently coming to the end of pork fat she clarified two years ago. Her house bears the brunt of 90°F in high summer and as the 'cave' is damp, the toupines are not stored in an especially cool place. Goose fat melts at a lower temperature than pork fat and needs to be boiled up now and then, even if kept in cool conditions. However, since it is unlikely that la Cuisine Périgourdine will make a daily appearance on the table of the busy British housewife, a one-litre tin of goose fat should suffice the yearly needs of even an enthusiast, and the tin can be kept in the refrigerator. Both goose fat and walnut oil can be bought in high-class grocers in Great Britain.

THE PLACE OF GARLIC IN LA CUISINE PÉRIGOURDINE

If for you hell and garlic are synonymous then I suggest you give this book away and go back to fish-fingers and baked beans. Even the French from other regions click their tongues over the quantities of garlic used in Périgord, but the soil here produces a species of the condiment which is larger and less strong than elsewhere. The cloves are planted during the young moons of January and February or at the full moon in March, and if you think that is mumbo-jumbo, try planting garlic at intervals from January to April and see which produces the best crop. The individual characteristics of the local garlic is the first argument in defence of its lavish use. The second is that in most cases it is left to simmer so long that it impregnates the other ingredients to the point where it is only discernible as a 'perfume' to the dish. If your reaction to a sauce is to open your mouth and flap your hand, the cook has failed.

'A little garlic and a little parsley' is the catch-phrase of the region, and I can recommend the immediate purchase of a mortar and pestle. The method best suited to get the greatest enhancement of these two flavours is to crush cloves of garlic with several heads of fresh parsley until the juices of both are thoroughly blended. French beans, tomatoes and carrots, to name only three vegetables, are made exquisite by the adition of pounded garlic and parsley just before serving.

I will not enlarge here on the therapeutic virtues attached to garlic, other than to say it is claimed it stimulates the memory, develops articulate expression, cures some infectious diseases and is a distributor of vitamins. I have been unable to make an assessment of these claims as the necessary dose exceeds that habitually imbibed by this population.

The French are essentially ritualists and their need for clearly defined methods and styles extends to their likes and dislikes in cooking. The British are spontaneous innovators, but this does not mean that spontaneous combustion should be tolerated in *La Cuisine Britannique*. Ritual has the advantage over spontaneity only in that it raises the odds on success if you are not an instinctive cook.

A region that produces in abundance and unsurpassable quality all that nature has to offer gastronomic man must also produce superlative cooks, and it may be thought that the cooks of less richly endowed countries have no hope of achieving an equal standard of culinary art. However, today's markets and transport systems allow every one of us to challenge the Périgordines with a *Sauce Périgeux* or a *Confit de Porc*. It is true that the women here seem to know by instinct how to retain and enhance the quality of the wonderful ingredients available to them; it is true that, though they may not take longer than other women to prepare a meal, they are never less than perfectionist in its preparation, but there is nothing in the art of la Cuisine Périgourdine that cannot be attained outside the region.

NOTE

Since this is a book on Périgourdine cookery the recipes have been grouped to follow the sequence of a typical Périgourdin meal.

It is beyond the intended scope of this book to explain the techniques of fine French cookery – certain terms are more succinct in French than in English – however a glossary will be found at the end of this book. Some words have no English equivalent and, where such are unavoidable, the closest meaning follows in brackets.

WEIGHTS, MEASURES, SERVINGS AND TIMING

Shortly before going to print I was asked by the editor to specify exactly what was meant by 'a little water', 'as many minnows as you think people will eat', 'Cook until you judge it to be ready'. The demand brought the thirty-year-old shock wave from discovering *packet soups* in a remote jungle village in Central America welling to the surface and spilling over the rim of my subconscious. Uniformity, Standardization, Rigidity are the bane of creativity.

> And art, made tongue-tied by authority,
> And folly, doctor-like, controlling skill ...

To my mind, not only would it be folly to quantify 'a little water', or the precise time a piece of meat will take to cook, it would wreck every principle of *La Cuisine Périgourdine*. 'Mme Robert', one of the finest local cooks, has neither kitchen scales nor a measuring glass – she is typical of hundreds of other good cooks in the region.

Well, I have done my best to comply with the editor's request – and I feel as if I have betrayed a friend on the rack. As you ladle, pour and measure out your ingredients keep the word 'about' pulsing through your mind. No one but you can specify exactly the capacity of *your* tablespoon or the speed of *your* gas flame, and I can only tell you that you will get *about*:

> 2–3 centilitres per liqueur glass
> 6–8 centilitres per sherry or Madeira glass
> 10–12 centilitres per Bordeaux wineglass
> 18 centilitres per large wineglass
> 20 centilitres per tumbler.

Remember that every meal you serve is a *new* meal. Perhaps the meat won't be quite the same quality as the meat you bought last week, the runner-beans could be exhausted at the end of the season, the bottle of Médoc may be a different year. It is the spontaneity of cooking that makes it so exciting! Don't expect to make exactly the same dish every time you make *that* dish – are your three children exactly alike? And yet, you used the same ingredients!

There are various words used for a soup in Périgord, *la soupe, le potage*, and *le tourin* or *tourrain* being those most commonly used to differentiate between soup types.

La soupe is substantial, almost a meal in itself.

Le potage is often sieved or blended and is *never* served over bread.

Le tourin/tourrain is lighter, thinner than the other two, usually contains some onion or garlic and may be served over bread. 'Give me a succinct substitute for the word "tourin" ', I asked Monsieur Tonneau. 'Give me a succinct substitute for "le weekend" ', he replied. So I am forced to use the word 'tourin' in the subtitles of the recipes.

My own preference is for the ancient word *'la sobronade'*. Only the 90-year-old Mme Tuyot could tell me that it meant *'la soupe'*.

Alors, Allez! A la Sobronade!

In the heart of the French there is only room for France. One may be impatient with their contempt or pity for anyone not lucky enough to have been born a French man or woman, but here in Périgord the attitude is forgivable. Except that Périgord is not the left-centre of the French body, one might well call it her heart. It is here that one observes that ineffable taste, *goût, parfum*, flavour that is understood in all our minds as *'la vie française'*. Nowhere else do earth, water and air come together to cast such a spell over the senses. In few other places is modern man so drawn into nature. In Périgord, as elsewhere, the tractor has taken over from the ox, the motor-car from the horse, but nowhere else is man so strangely unchanged by what is known as 'progress'.

A Parisian who had made his home in Périgord wrote that the people were the poorest he had ever encountered; and the most courteous. The meaning of poverty differs in the city, of course, and though it is true that there are areas of France where agriculture is more profitable, the real quality of life in a region lies in something other than the number of tractors per farm or of fattened cattle at market. It is hardly surprising that, from the moment the Périgordin child is on solids, heaven and the kitchen become synonymous. Everything needed for his nourishment grows here to perfection –

every imaginable vegetable, over 300 species of edible fungi and mushroom including the famous truffle, delicious freshwater fish, luscious poultry and many kinds of game. No wonder heaven and food go mouth-to-mouth! No wonder the moment one utters the name of Périgord one is aware that man's sensuality has become centred in the mouth, *en route* for the stomach – and that sensuality begins with a soup.

The ambiguous phrase *'plat de résistance'*, meaning both that one could exist on the dish and that it might be the only existing dish must certainly be applied to *la soupe* in Périgord. In every region of France the evening meal begins with a soup, but in Périgord most people eat soup twice a day, while robust feeders like M. Tonneau (who claims that a good soup taken three times daily provides the body with all the water other than 'eau'-de-vie that it requires) replace morning coffee or chocolate by a broth (*bouillon*). In Périgord, no matter how grand or simple the meal, it begins with a soup – and its place in the life of the region may be gauged by the fact that one goes to *'la soupe'* (*'Allez! A la soupe!'*) when one goes to eat, no matter which meal is served.

Women here are assessed on the quality of their soups and in a region where, young and old, they seem to have been born with a tureen and ladle in the hand, for a woman to be told she makes a good soup is praise indeed.

The nourishing and morale-raising value of a good soup need not be stressed. Traditionally, the most substantial soups, whether based on beans, salted pork or vegetables, are thick enough to support a spoon upright in the tureen. These are soups to be eaten with a spoon and fork, particularly if the teeth are bad, the usual method being to crush the vegetables in the spoon with the fork. The liquid from the soup is reserved for the time-honoured custom, *le chabrol*, a ritual followed even by sophisticated diners in smart restaurants: while there are still a few spoonfuls of warm bouillon in the bottom of the plate, a glass of red wine is poured into it – the peasants say 'enough to cover the spoon', in horizontal mode, one presumes – and this mixture is drunk from the bowl itself. It is said that the warm broth develops the 'tonic' properties of the alcohol.

Whether in a farmhouse kitchen or a respected restaurant, almost all soups are served over stale bread, sliced thinly into the bottom of the tureen. Most newcomers to this practice see it as a symbol of poverty or avarice but in fact the Périgordins *like* wet bread. Any amount of wet bread is consumed in Périgord, from dishes of subtlety and refinement served on bread soddened by their rich sauces to 'le trampi', taken between four and five of an afternoon, when a man's energies are flagging. Le trampi consists of bread sprinkled with sugar and soaked with red or white wine – a stimulant considered too invigorating for persons subject to blood-pressure problems.

All the recipes in this book are authentic to the region and though, in principle, to leave out or to add an ingredient will be to detract from that authenticity, no soup will be worsened by the absence of bread.

LA FRICASSÉE

No matter what else goes into a soup, what meat, vegetables or stock, in Périgord one adds a 'fricassée' to the rest. The fricassée consists of vegetables removed from the soup half an hour before the end of cooking (or occasionally raw vegetables) to be browned gently in goose or pork fat. When the vegetables are nicely browned, a spoonful of flour is sprinkled over them, they are moistened with a little stock and left to thicken and simmer a few moments before the fricassée is returned to the soup pot.

The excellence of Périgourdine soups is largely due to the flavour this fricassé gives to the other ingredients. The essence of the method lies in knowing which of the vegetables being cooked will be best for the fricassée: it is not simply a question of browning all the vegetables. I have no absolute guidelines to offer: it seems to depend on that ephemeral knowledge already cited, innate in the women of this region – but the vegetables most often fricasséed are celeriac, onions and root vegetables (other than potatoes). Sometimes lardons (see glossary) are browned separately and added just before the soup is served, but with time to allow the rest of the soup to take their flavour

Note: There is a noticeable difference in flavour between sautéeing the raw vegetables before you make a soup and in removing selected vegetables for a fricassée towards the end of the cooking.

The first soup here was made for me recently by Mme Robert, a woman of a thousand learned skills and certain unlearnable gifts such as intuition, perception and compassion. There are several versions of the tourin (Madame Robert made me the simple *Tourin Blanchi* which follows) and the most curious version is that served either at the beginning or at the end of a wedding: a tradition still in current practice. The wedding tourin has so much pepper in it that it seems to have been made of earth. At its first appearance it is served to guests arriving at the house – no guest may set foot across the threshold until he or she has eaten a mouthful, but of course there is someone at hand with a brimming glass to soothe the burning tongue. At its second appearance, it is inflicted on the just-bedded couple, who are forced to drink the tourin before being dragged from the bed to show the company their sheets. Mme Robert's only daughter was forced to drink the pepper soup from the flowered porcelain potty she had used as a baby, kept over the years for that very purpose.

Le Tourin Blanchi (1)

Time: 30 minutes
Serves 6–8

1 tbsp goose, duck or pork fat
4 large cloves of garlic
1 tbsp plain flour
3 pt (1.5 l) water, heated in a
    saucepan

1 tbsp wine vinegar or verjuice
1 egg, separated
Salt and pepper
Handful of vermicelli (optional)

Slice the cloves of garlic finely and brown gently in the fat. Blend in the flour and thin gradually with a little of the hot water (about half a pint). Season and allow to simmer for 10 minutes.

Tip the contents of the pan into the saucepan of hot water, bring to the boil and reduce heat. Drop the egg white into the soup and leave to cook. When firm, chop the white into small dice, and return to the soup. Toss in a handful of vermicelli a few minutes before the end of cooking if required. Put the yolk into the tureen and blend with the spoonful of vinegar or verjuice. Gradually pour the hot soup into the tureen, mixing in the egg yolk as you do so.

Traditionally this tourin is served over bread but it does go well with vermicelli.

Le Tourin Blanchi (2)

Time: 45 minutes
Serves 6–8

This soup is made exactly as the previous soup but 3 large onions, sliced, are substituted for the garlic.

Le Tourin à l'Oseille
(Sorrel tourin)

Time: 30–40 minutes
Serves 6–8

1 tbsp goose, duck or pork fat
1 lb (500g) potatoes, peeled
2 good handfuls of sorrel,
   washed and coarsely chopped
1 tbsp plain flour
3 pt (1.5 l) salted water

1 egg, separated
1 large clove of garlic, sliced
½ pt (300 ml) milk
Salt and pepper
Chervil and sorrel to garnish

Boil the potatoes in the salted water. When cooked, crush them in the water with a fork. Heat the fat in a frying-pan and gently brown the garlic. Throw in the sorrel leaves, sprinkle over the flour, add the egg white and moisten the whole with a little of the potato water. Add the contents of the frying-pan to the potato saucepan and heat gently.

Bring the milk to the boil. Put the egg yolk into a tureen and blend in the milk. Carefully pour the potato-and-sorrel soup into the tureen. Just before serving, sprinkle finely chopped chervil and sorrel onto the soup.

Note: Wholemeal croûtons fried in goose fat go well with this.

Le Tourin aux Tomates
(Tomato tourin)

Time: 40 mins
Serves 8

1 tbsp goose, duck or pork fat
1 large onion, sliced
4 large cloves garlic, sliced
1 lb (550 g) tomatoes, peeled and
   quartered

1 tbsp plain flour
4 pt (2 l) water
Salt and pepper
Small handful of vermicelli

Melt the fat and gently brown the onions and garlic. Add the tomatoes and leave to cook for ten minutes.

In a second pan bring the water to the boil and season. Empty the tomato mixture into the water and continue cooking for 20–30 minutes. Towards the end of the cooking time toss in some fine vermicelli.

La Soupe aux Ecrevisses
(Freshwater crayfish soup)

Time: 1 hour
Serves 8–10

1 tbsp goose or pork fat	Bouquet garni
The white of 1 or 2 good leeks, sliced in rounds	12 crayfish with shells
	4 pt (2 l) water
2 onions, sliced	2 glasses white wine – Mont-
1 carrot, cut in rounds	bazillac or Entre Deux Mers
1 tbsp plain flour	1 or 2 egg yolks
Salt and pepper	

To serve: ½ a garlic clove and one slice of bread per person

Put the water on to heat in a saucepan. In a separate pan melt the fat and gently brown the chopped onions, leeks and carrots. Dust with the flour and thicken carefully with a little hot water. Tip the vegetable mixture into the saucepan of water.

Clean the crayfish, removing the bitter portion from the tail by taking hold of the middle section of the tail and pulling. The bitter portion should come away easily. (Or ask your fishmonger to do it for you.) Reserve the shells and tails. Heat the white wine and set alight. Cook the crayfish in the wine until they are a good red colour. Lift them out on to a clean cloth and keep warm. Add the wine they have been cooked in to the vegetables.

Crush the shells and tails of the crayfish in a mortar and pestle and add to the soup. Cook fairly fast for 30 minutes.

To serve: Strain the soup and thicken a little with the yolks of one or two eggs. Lightly rub halved cloves of garlic over some slices of bread, and putting the bread and the fish into the tureen, pour the slightly thickened liquid over the top.

La Soupe à la Citrouille
(Pumpkin soup)

Time: 1½ hours
Serves 8–10

4 pt (2 l) hot water
4 oz (125 g) onions, chopped
1 knob goose or pork fat
8 oz (250 g) tomatoes, peeled and
    quartered
2 large cloves garlic, crushed
Salt, pepper and bouquet garni

12 oz (375 g) potatoes, peeled and
    diced
1 lb (500 g) pumpkin, peeled,
    deseeded and cubed
12 oz (375 g) mangetout,
    chopped
Small bunch chopped chives
Croûtons, fried in goose fat

Place the onions and the goose or pork fat in a pan and allow to sweat. Add the tomatoes, garlic and bouquet garni and seasoning. Cook gently for 10 minutes. Gradually stir in the water and leave to simmer for a further 10 minutes.

Add the potatoes, pumpkin and mangetout. Bring to the boil, reduce heat and simmer gently for 1 hour.

To serve: Snip the chives finely into the bottom of the tureen and pour the soup over them. Garnish with croûtons.

La Mique
(Maize dumpling)

La Mique is one of the oldest recipes in Périgord. Maize grows very vigorously in this soil and, in addition to being the staple food for fattening pigs and poultry, is the principal grain used in the force-feeding of geese for pâté de foie gras. Man has also made use of the grain for himself, grinding it for its flour, and at one time maize bread was the only bread the Périgordins ate: an unleavened flat bread called '*la fougeasse*'. For them la mique was essential to their nourishment since bread made from wheat was considered a luxury. Nowadays maize flour is somewhat despised, though recently I saw prepacked (*quel horreur!*) maize miques on sale in one of our mobile shops. Les miques are very easy to make:

They can be served warm with a main course such as jugged hare or rabbit, or cool as a dessert (see page 172).

Time: 30 minutes
Makes 3 substantial miques

8 oz (250 g) maize flour
8 oz (250 g) plain flour
1 wineglass of tepid water

1 tbsp goose fat
Salt

Mix the two flours together thoroughly. Stir in the salt, rub in the fat and bind with the water to make a stiff dough. Divide the dough into 3 and with floured hands form into balls about the size of an orange.

In a large saucepan bring to the boil enough water to cover the miques well. Drop the miques into the boiling water, turning them about to cook evenly for about half an hour.

Drain.

La Soupe aux Miques et aux Choux et Petit Salé
(Maize dumplings in salt pork and cabbage soup)

Time: 2½–3 hours
Serves 6–8

1 large or 2 small good-hearted
    cabbages
A piece of pickled pork or salted
    knuckle
1 small celeriac, chopped
1 small turnip, diced

6 carrots, sliced
2 large onions, chopped
2 good leeks, sliced
Salt and pepper
Bouquet garni
1 lb (500 g) miques (see p. 26)

Separate the cabbage leaves and blanch in boiling water. Put all the ingredients into a large saucepan with enough water to cover. Bring to the boil, skim and leave to simmer for 2 hours. Adjust the seasoning.

Prepare 1 lb (500 g) of miques as in the previous recipe, but cook them in the soup for 30 minutes.

Before serving removed some carrots and celeriac from the soup and fricassée in a frying-pan as described on page 22. Return to the soup 10 minutes before serving to flavour the dish in the traditional Périgourdin style.

La Soupe à la Queue de Boeuf
(Oxtail soup)

Time: 2½–3 hours
Serves 6–8

1 oxtail
2 large or 3 small leeks, sliced
1 small turnip, diced
Heart of a cabbage, diced

3 or 4 sticks of celery, sliced
Salt, pepper and 2 cloves
Other vegetables of your choice

Chop the tail into portions about 6 in (18 cm) long. Tie together like faggots and put to soak in lukewarm water for at least an hour before cooking. Drain, and put into a casserole or saucepan with enough water to cover. Bring to the boil and cook for 1 hour, skimming from time to time.

Add vegetables, the cloves and seasoning. Continue cooking for 1½ hours, topping up the broth if it has reduced too much.

While the meat is still hot, remove from the bones and set aside to serve as an excellent entrèe (see page 47).

Note: To my mind, oxtail soup is better reheated. Allow to chill, so that the solidified fat can be easily removed to leave the juices clear for reheating.

La Soupe aux Abattis de Volaille
(Giblet soup)

Midwinter is the time for making conserves of goose, duck and turkey – 'les confits'. Only the choicest cuts of the birds are tinned or bottled, but nothing is wasted. Carcasses, necks, feet, wings and giblets are put on sale side by side with the pieces to be conserved. The butcher will sell you a pack containing the neck, feet, wings and giblets of a goose for about Ffr10, which will make an excellent soup for 4.

'You will' (I am told), 'come to the pleasure of nuzzling the wings and neck, of sucking the feet ("*pas mal du tout!*", not bad at all!), of opening the head with a strong, sharp knife to impale the tiny brain that will amaze the palate when eaten on a piece of country bread.' And there you are! From 'almost nothing', a meal for a gourmet.

Time: 2–2½ hours
Serves 4

1 'abattis' pack (i.e. the neck, feet, wings and giblets of a goose)
heart of 1 cabbage, quartered
3 leeks, sliced in rounds
3 or 4 sticks of celery, sliced
Salt and pepper
2 cloves
To serve: slices of wholemeal bread

Burn off any remaining plumage with a spill. Remove any tough skins. Cut the head from the neck close to the head. Cut the neck into portions. Discard the claws and thoroughly clean all the pieces. Put the cleaned pieces into a saucepan with water to cover and bring to the boil. Skim. Add the vegetables and other ingredients. Cook slowly for 2 hours.

To serve: Sprinkle pepper over slices of wholemeal bread in the bottom of your tureen and pour the soup over.

Le Farci
(Stuffing balls)

Much use is made of stuffings in Périgord: meat, poultry, fish and vegetables all have their recipes and a selection of each will be found in this book. The following recipe is the most traditional, almost, one might say, the archetypal Périgourdin stuffing. *Le farci* is a little like dumplings in use, but is larger and usually cooked in the soup.

It is the custom for the man of the house to slice *le farci* – a purely symbolic gesture since the women have done all the important work. There is such significance in this tradition that in a household ruled by a woman, where we would say 'she wears the trousers', they say 'One can see who slices *le farci* in that household!'

Time: 30 minutes
Serves 4, with soup

2 oz (50 g) streaky bacon, finely chopped
1 large clove garlic, sliced
Salt and pepper

Small handful parsley, chopped
4 oz (125 g) stale breadcrumbs
1–2 eggs, beaten
1 large cabbage leaf

Mix salt, pepper and chopped parsley into the breadcrumbs. Add the chopped bacon and garlic and bind with beaten egg.

Clean a large cabbage leaf. Cut out the hardest part of the stalk and blanch to soften. Wrap the farci mixture in the cabbage leaf, tie firmly with string and place in your soup pot to cook for 30 minutes. Before serving remove the farci from the soup, cut the string, discard the cabbage leaf and slice the stuffing. Serve a portion to each person and pour the soup over it.

La Potée Périgourdine

This is rather hard to translate, but it means, roughly, a potful or jugful of something.

M. Tonneau tells me that *la Potée* was served in very cold weather during '*la Chasse*', a custom that he hasn't seen for forty years. The shooting season may have continued into winter forty years ago – it is now limited to certain days only in early autumn and a game licence for even this short period is over £100 per gun. The licence fee may have had more to do with the lapse of the tradition of serving *la Potée* than the shorter mildish hunting season.

Time: 3 hours
Serves 8–10

2 lb (1 kg) pickled pork	1 large onion pierced with a clove
1 large Saucisson de Ménage (or an unsliced salami)	3 large cloves of garlic
6 saveloys	Thyme and parsley
1 large white cabbage	A few potatoes
3 carrots	3 turnips
3 leeks	Any other vegetables in season (e.g. celeriac and celery)
A small swede	

First buy a very big pot, and be careful with the salt here: the meats will be salty enough.

Trim off the stalk of the cabbage, cut into quarters and blanch in boiling water. Prepare all the vegetables and cut in large dice. Put the cabbage and all the other vegetables except the potatoes into your large pot. Add the herbs, garlic and seasoning and pickled pork. Cover with water and cook over a low heat for 2 hours. Add the saucisson or salami, the saveloys, and the potatoes cut into quarters. Continue cooking for 45 minutes.

This very substantial soup usually has *le farci* added at the same time as the potatoes. The farci is taken out just before serving, removed from the cabbage leaf, sliced and returned to reheat in the soup without further cooking.

La Potée, followed by a crisp green salad, cheese and fruit, and helped down with a rich red Cahors, makes a meal to remember.

Soupe à la Carcasse de Dinde ou d'Oie
(Soup from turkey or goose carcass)

I am including this soup for the enthusiast.

When one is making the preserves of turkey or goose meat (*les confits*) one is left with the carcasses. Rub them with salt and put into covered earthenware crocks for several days. With these carcasses, or pieces of carcass, one can make a very good vegetable soup, using whatever vegetables are in season. For those who enjoy their game high, these salted carcasses do indeed add *quelque chose* ... for others, this could be *la soupe* to end all soupes.

Bouillon or Pot au Feu de Périgord

I have left *the* soup to end all soups to the last. It is a Périgourdin pot au feu and it demonstrates to perfection how an elaborate menu may be effected with the least drain on time, tempers and energy: a soup *and* four different meat courses being cooked in the same huge pot.

Le Pot au Feu is familiar to most cooks interested in recipes from other countries, if only by name. It is the countryman's answer to catering for a family gathering: finding four meats is no problem in the country where most people have hens and a pig, and where mutton and veal can be bought as whole slaughtered animals ready for the deep freeze or other forms of conserving. In Périgord it is considered bad form not to give your guests something bought, and since poultry, veal, pork, lamb and all charcuterie, confits and pâtés are home produced, to buy a joint of beef for the Pot au Feu is a mark of respect for the guests.

It is said that everyone is related one way or another in Périgord, and, since it is almost obligatory to invite the remotest relations along with one's friends and neighbours, it is not unusual to find more than a hundred round the long table set up in the barn. The scene may be imagined: the table glisteningly covered with an immaculate cloth and finely caparisoned with cutlery, glassware, baskets of fruit and bottles.

In Périgord, the barn and cow stalls are under the same roof, but separated by beautifully carved 'crèches' or head stalls. The stable floor is lower than the barn and cobbled with tooth-shaped pebbles driven into the earth. Of their own accord, the cows turn their heads at a slant to pass their horns through the stall opening, and there they are, gazing ruminatively on the wedding feast, munching the mounds of hay pushed up to their heads now level with the barn floor. Often the stalls themselves are garlanded with flowers and the cattle are framed in a veritable Garden of Eden – another striking example of Périgordin man's rapport with nature, an embellishment of the Périgordin idyll.

Time: 3–4 hours
Serves a multitude

2 lb (1 kg) silverside or topside of beef
3 lb (1.5 kg) lean veal
2 lb (1 kg) veal or pork bones or a mixture
1 knucklebone of veal
1 chicken
1 smallish turkey
As many onions, carrots, turnips leeks and celery as you think fit, cleaned and diced (say 4 good-sized onions, 1 lb (500 g) carrots, 1 small turnips, 4 leeks, 4 sticks celery)
8 large cloves of garlic
A sprig of thyme, a bunch of parsley and 2 or 3 bay leaves
Salt and pepper
1 clove to be stuck into the onion

For the farci:

4 oz (125 g) stale breadcrumbs	1 egg
2 oz (50 g) ham or bacon, chopped	[and a *very* large pot]

Make sure all the meats are securely tied or trussed because they will be in the simmering liquid a long time. Stick a clove of garlic into the beef and put it, the bones and the rest of the garlic cloves into the pot. Add enough cold water to cover by about 6 inches (18 cms) and bring to the boil. Skim, put in all the seasonings and herbs, and simmer for 1 hour.

Stuff the chicken with a 'farci' of breadcrumbs, ham or bacon and an egg. (In Périgord a very salty raw ham is used.) Put it, also, into the pot and add the veal, the knucklebone and the turkey and continue simmering for a further 2 hours. Skim during this time. After 2 hours put in all the vegetables and continue cooking for another 1½ to 2 hours until you judge all is ready. The liquid will have diminished, of course, but take care if adding further water not to overdo it. The bouillon must be a rich blend of all the juices.

There is nothing particularly Périgourdin about this method, except, perhaps, the lavish use of garlic (but the garlic will merely have given a perfume to the whole and you need not be alarmed by the quantity used). The influence of Périgord comes out at the moment of serving.

To serve:
1 Strain the liquid, skim off any fat, and thicken if wished with a little vermicelli. Serve with croûtons of bread rubbed with garlic.
2 Serve an hors d'œuvre: a tomato salad would be refreshing.
3 Make a *Sauce Périgueux* (page 117). Carve the beef and the veal and serve with the *Sauce Périgueux* poured over the slices.
4 Make a mushroom sauce. Carve the chicken and turkey and serve with the sauce.
5 Serve a fresh green salad with walnut oil dressing.
6 A selection of cheeses.
7 Beignets (fritters, see page 169).
8 Coffee and liqueurs.

LES ENTRÉES
— Entrées —

Comprising:

Les hors d'œuvres (Hors d'Œuvres)
Les omelettes (Omelettes)
Les œufs (Egg Dishes)
Les Plats Composés (Made-up Dishes)
Les Escargots (Snails)
Les Entrées de Poisson (Fish Entrées)
Les Pâtés (Pâtés)

The Oxford Dictionary definition of the word 'entrée' is: 'a dish served between the fish and meat courses'. This would not do in Périgord, and here Mme Tonneau's astonished stare and explosive cry of, 'Why do the English have to be so different?', is justified. I don't know why we call the dish between the fish and the meat an entrée, unless we look upon that dish as opening the door on the serious business of the meal. Viewed rationally, since *la soupe* opens every meal in Périgord, the entrée should be *la soupe*, but in fact *les entrées* come after *la soupe*.

There are numerous sorts of entrée, principally based on the truffle and foie gras, several of which may be served at an elaborate meal and at least two at an ordinary lunch. It is difficult to be precise as to the order of serving the various entrées, this being to some extent a matter decided by choice or availability of ingredients, so I have set out the recipes in the sequence most commonly encountered.

Les Hors d'Œuvres

The hors d'œuvres, in the generally accepted sense, are recruited from whatever fresh vegetables are in season, and are not much different from hors d'œuvres elsewhere in France, only their dressing or garnish giving them their taste of Périgord.

Les Jeunes Artichauts à la Moutarde
(Young globe artichokes with mustard)

Young raw globe artichokes are delicious as an hors d'œuvre. Choose them when they are not much bigger than a walnut.

A couple of dozen young globe artichokes. The amount will naturally depend on the number catered for. Proportions for the dressing are:

1 tbsp French mustard
3–4 tbsp walnut oil
Salt and pepper

Cut off the pointed top of the artichoke leaves. Gently open the leaves to form a flower and arrange the artichokes in the form of a crown in an hors d'œuvres dish containing a little chilled salted water or water and vinegar. Work the mustard and walnut oil into a smooth sauce or dip, seasoning to taste.

La Salade de Tomates à l'Eau-de-vie
(Tomato salad in eau-de-vie)

Time: Allow several hours to marinate the tomatoes

4 good-sized ripe but firm tomatoes	3 tbsp walnut oil
1 tbsp eau-de-vie or alcohol at least 45% with no flavour	A little finely chopped raw onion or chives as a garnish, finely chopped
1 tbsp wine vinegar	Salt and ground black pepper

Wash and dry the tomatoes. Cut them into quarters or slices, taking care to remove the pips and expelling a little of the juice. Leave them to stand for several hours with salt, pepper and the eau-de-vie. Turn them about gently from time to time. When the alcohol has thoroughly penetrated the tomatoes, make the dressing with the vinegar and walnut oil. Pour it over the tomatoes and move them about in it until they are well-covered. Garnish with very finely chopped raw onion or chives before serving.

La Salade de Concombres
(Cucumber salad)

Time: 24 hours to marinate the cucumber

Some people find cucumber indigestible, but a glass of good red wine taken with the salad will make it no more painful to the stomach than a crisp fresh lettuce. Taken as a balanced accompaniment to a meal, wine helps rather than hinders the digestion.

1 or 2 cucumbers	Sea salt and pepper
1 tbsp vinegar	Chopped onion or chives
3–4 tbsp walnut oil	Parsley or green pimento

Cucumbers should not be yellow for this sort of salad, but a good fresh green colour all the way through. Cut the cucumbers in half lengthways and remove the seeds. Slice them as finely as possible into a dish, sprinkle with sea salt (*gros sel*) and leave to stand for 24 hours.

Drain and wipe, put into a clean dish and make a dressing with the oil and vinegar, a little pepper but NO SALT. Pour the dressing over the cucumbers, turning the slices in the dressing. Garnish with finely chopped onions or chives, parsley or green pimento.

Les Poireaux à la Vinaigrette
(Leeks in oil and vinegar)

Apart from being indispensable in soups and stews, leeks are not much used in Périgord other than in this fashion. Eaten as an hors d'œuvre, they have much the same flavour as asparagus.

Time: 20 minutes for cooking the leeks and enough time for them to go cold

As many leeks as you need per person	Chopped parsley to garnish
1 tbsp vinegar to 3–4 tbsp walnut oil	Salt and pepper

Choose young, thin leeks. Cut them in equal lengths and tie in bundles. Put to cook in boiling water. Drain. Cut the string and allow to get cold.

Make the dressing from the oil and vinegar, adding salt and pepper to taste. Put the leeks in a dish, pour the dressing over and garnish with chopped parsley.

La Salade de Tomates et Haricots Verts
(Tomato and French bean salad)

3 or 4 large firm tomatoes	3–4 tbsp walnut oil
8 oz (250 g) cooked French beans	Salt and pepper
1 tbsp vinegar	A little finely chopped raw onion

Wash and dry the tomatoes. Slice finely and put in a dish with the French beans cut to convenient lengths. Make the vinaigrette, season to taste and pour over the tomatoes and beans. Turn them about in the dressing. Just before serving garnish with finely chopped raw onion.

Les Fèves à la Vinaigrette
(Broad beans in dressing)

The Périgordins make inventive use of a good crop of vegetables, many of which are put into salads. 'Thinking ahead' is part and parcel of the Périgordin make-up – hence their fine conserves – and frequently more vegetables are cooked than will be needed for the meal in question, with an eye to an hors d'œuvre for the next day's lunch. Follow their example therefore; cook twice as many broad beans as you need for your lunch, and next day serve them as an hors d'œuvre à la vinaigrette, dressed with a little chopped onion or finely chopped pimento.

Two Other Popular Hors d'Œuvres in Périgord

Radishes
Both the large black and the small round red radish, eaten quite simply with bread and butter.

Melon
Both the cantaloup and the fine Terrasson, usually served with a sweet white wine.

Les Omelettes
(Omelettes)

After the soup and the hors d'œuvres, it is usual to serve either an omelette, a made-up entrée dish or pâté, and even, in some cases, all three. Omelettes are eaten all over the world but, naturally, the Périgordines have their own way of making them. They also have the pleasure of rediscovering regional fillings as the earth takes its course around the sun, of savouring fresh eggs perfumed by a sliver of truffle – a perfume so intense in season that one can scarcely remain beside a basket of freshly gathered truffles – or of enjoying the crispness of young *pissenlit* leaves (dandelions) tossed into the omelette at the last moment.

The principle of omelette-making here is not unlike the principle of tea-making in Britain. For a simple omelette – that is, an omelette without a filling – allow 2 eggs per person and 1 or 2 *under*: for 6 people one might use 10 eggs, for example. For an omelette filled with foie gras, cèpes or other vegetables allow 1 egg per person and 2 *over*.

L'Omelette aux Truffes
(Truffle omelette)

The price of truffles being so high, some people use only truffle peelings for an omelette, but this is a false economy; by the time they have been reduced in cooking they have lost their quintessential flavour. Much better to use the entire truffle, particularly for an omelette for 6 people (and, if you can afford it, the ideal would be 2 truffles).

Time: A few minutes
Serves 6

8 eggs	2 truffles
Salt and pepper	A knob of goose fat

Wash and clean the truffles by brushing them thoroughly. Peel and cut into thin slices. Beat the eggs vigorously with a little salt and pepper. Chop the truffle peelings and add to the beaten eggs. Heat some goose fat in a pan, drop the truffle slices in and allow them to impregnate the fat with their 'parfum'. Remove them fairly quickly before they have a chance to cook and add them to the beaten eggs.

Reheat the goose fat, drop in the egg-and-truffle mixture and cook quickly, turning in a spiral fashion with a fork. Serve at once.

L'Omelette Périgourdine aux Cèpes
(Cèpe omelette)

Mushroom omelette is a celebrated dish, but the Périgord cèpe omelette has become especially celebrated.

Time: method 1 – 20 minutes; method 2 – 30 minutes
Serves 4–5

1 lb (500 g) cèpes
Salt and pepper
Goose fat and walnut oil for

cooking the cèpes
1 garlic clove crushed with
    parsley

If you are using fresh cèpes there is no need to peel them. Cut the stalk off just underneath the cap. Do not discard the stalks. Wash the cèpes in several changes of water and leave to stand for 30 minutes in the last rinsing water. Drain, and stand on a clean cloth. Slice.
    The cèpes can be dealt with in one of two ways.

Method 1
Plunge the cèpes into boiling, salted water for a few moments, just long enough for the water to change colour and to become slightly bitter. Drain and dry on a clean cloth.

Method 2
This method is preferred by those who hold that to boil the cèpes spoils their flavour and aroma. Fry the cèpes in a mixture of half goose fat, half walnut oil.

Whichever method you choose (and you may also choose tinned cèpes), you come to the point where the sliced cèpes will be fried in a mixture of half goose fat, half walnut oil. (If you are using tinned cèpes this is where you begin and end, as you only need to heat them through.)
    Having cleaned the cèpes and started to cook them in the manner of your choice, turn your attention to the stalks. Cut off the earth end and chop the stalks finely. Pound the garlic and parsley in a mortar and pestle, add to the chopped stalks and incorporate into the pan where the sliced cèpes are cooking.
    Beat the eggs briskly. Remove the pan from the heat, take out the cèpes mixture and add to the beaten eggs, continuing to beat. Season.
    Reheat the fat in the pan, pour in the omelette mixture and cook over a brisk flame, turning it in on itself either with a spatula or with little shakes of the pan. Serve immediately.

L'Omelette aux Boutons de Scorsonères
(Scorzonera/black salsify omelette)

This is one of the best omelettes there is in Périgord. Scorzonera is wild salsify, or black salsify. The buds of the plant, fried gently and put into an omelette, have something of the flavour of asparagus – 'something the flavour of', being the nearest one can come to describing their individual delicacy. If you don't know the plant, now is the moment to identify it: it is a very rich resource for the enthusiastic cook, both the roots and the buds being usable, and since it sprouts like a weed in most vegetable gardens, the cost is no more than the energy required to step out of the kitchen door to pick it. Packets of scorzonera buds can be bought in supermarkets throughout France. If no fresh source is available, it is worth urging your local greengrocer to stock up from his European Community wholesaler.

For this recipe you need to gather the buds before they have opened into yellow flowers. The tighter the buds, the better they will be.

Time: A few minutes, plus 1 hour to soak buds

As many eggs as you require (see page 37)
A handful of scorzonera buds each

1 tbsp vinegar
A knob of goose fat
Salt and pepper

Soak the buds in water and vinegar for about 1 hour. Rinse, and drain on a clean cloth. Heat some goose fat in a pan and when it begins to sing, toss in the buds, turning them from time to time with a fork. IMPORTANT – the flavour will be spoilt if they over-cook. Remove from the heat and keep hot.

Beat your eggs and season. Add the buds, still beating. Make your omelette in the usual way and serve immediately.

Note: Mme Tuyot, our Grande Cuisinière, tells me that she has never met anyone tasting this omelette for the first time who has not pronounced it a Work of Culinary Art.

L'Omelette à la Graisse de Foie Gras
(Goose fat omelette)

At first sight, the name of this omelette may cause one to recoil, but the fat surrounding pâtés and terrines of foie gras is full of little pieces of liver, meat and truffle and can be used in many different ways. It lends itself perfectly to this omelette.

Time: A few minutes

As many eggs as you require (see page 37)
The fat from a pâté de foie gras

Pepper, allspice and be sparing the salt

Heat the fat. Beat your eggs and add the heated fat to them. Beat together briskly, seasoning with pepper and allspice. Put the pan back on a hot flame, pour in the egg-and-fat mixture and make the omelette in the usual way.

Note: This omelette goes very well with a good red Bordeaux or a red Bergerac.

L'Omelette aux Gardêches
(Minnow omelette)

The 'gardêche' is not included in French dictionaries: it is the Périgordin word for *'vairon'* – 'minnow' to us – and many weeks passed before I finally traced the *French* name for the fish.

The minnow is too small to be cooked individually, but could be cooked in the manner of whitebait, in a batter. In Périgord, it is only served in omelettes or (as it is curiously called) in an 'omelette without eggs' – a term indicating the final look of the dish in which the fish stick together to form a mass.

The minnow may be tiny, but this physical disadvantage has its compensations in the largeness of its stupidity: it doesn't take long to catch enough minnows for a good-sized omelette.

Time: A few minutes

As many eggs as you require (see page 37)	Salt and pepper
	Chopped chives and parsley
As many fish as you think each person will eat (usually 6 minnows each)	Plain flour for coating
	Oil for frying
	A knob of goose fat

Wash the fish thoroughly and dry with kitchen paper. There is no need to cut off their heads. Roll them in flour, heat the oil in a deep chip fryer and toss in the fish. When cooked, drain and keep hot. Season.

Make a simple omelette in the usual way. At the moment of folding it, put in the fish and fold the omelette over them. Serve garnished with chopped chives and parsley.

L'Omelette à l'Oseille
(Sorrel omelette)

Time: A few minutes

A good handful of fresh sorrel
As many eggs as you require (see page 37)

Salt and pepper
A knob of goose fat

Wash the sorrel thoroughly and chop finely. Beat the eggs with salt and pepper. Add the sorrel and continue beating. Heat the fat and make the omelette in the usual way.

If you prefer the sorrel cooked, fry it before adding to the eggs but make sure you use another pan for making the omelette as the sorrel gives an acid flavour to the pan.

Note: sorrel omelette is a very fresh, healthy omelette, particularly good for people who have lost their appetite for one reason or another.

L'Omelette de la Rouzille
(Mme Rouzille's omelette)

This omelette can be prepared very quickly and is most appetizing.

Time: A few minutes
Serves 4–5

6–8 fresh eggs
2 oz (50 g) grated cheese
Salt and pepper
Nutmeg, grated
A few chopped chives

A knob of goose fat
Enough sliced salami or other savoury sausage to decorate the platter

Beat the eggs, seasoning, a little grated nutmeg and chopped chives together for 10 minutes. Have ready the grated cheese, the sliced salami and a heated platter,

Heat the goose fat. Make the omelette, fold it on to itself and arrange on the heated platter. Trickle the grated cheese over it and arrange the salami all round the omelette.

Les Oeufs
(Egg Dishes)

The simple egg becomes a masterpiece in Périgord!

Les Oeufs à la Périgourdine
(Perigord eggs)

Instructions to take 'a little pâté de foie gras truffé' is on a par with Mrs Beeton's 'take two dozen eggs'; and, of course, in Périgord few housewives are without their home-made pâté. The above recipe can be equally good made with potted meat, 'rillettes' or 'grillons' being much cheaper (see page 114).

Time: 20–30 minutes

Eggs (see page 37)
1 tin or 6 oz (170 g) pâté de foie
   gras truffé (reserve the fat)

Salt and pepper
1–2 egg whites
A little chervil, chopped

Hard-boil the eggs. Shell them, cut them lengthwise and remove the yolks. Crush the yolks with some pâté de foie gras truffé and a little chopped chervil, salt and pepper. Fill the empty egg whites with this filling, dip each one in some beaten egg white and fry quickly in the fat that was round the pâté. Serve at once.

Les Oeufs à la Coque Cuit sous la Cendre

An egg à la coque means soft-boiled, but if you don't like runny eggs, simply leave them under the cinders for longer.

This is a very old recipe, but in a region where most people burn a wood fire of one sort or another, it is still practised, and gives the eggs a particularly delicious flavour.

Put freshly laid eggs into cold water for a few minutes, just to wet the shells. Then put them into the hearth surrounded by hot ash. In 4 or 5 minutes they will be cooked to perfection. Serve with fingers of bread crisply fried in walnut oil.

Les Oeufs Frits au Vin
(Fried eggs with wine sauce)

Time: 50 minutes

1 egg per person	Bread
Garlic	Red wine sauce (page 118)
Goose fat	

Prepare the red wine sauce. Rub some slices of bread with crushed garlic. Melt some goose fat in a pan, fry the slices of bread both sides and put aside to keep hot. Fry the eggs in the fat, also on both sides. Place an egg on each slice of garlic bread, cover with red wine sauce and serve immediately.

Les Oeufs à la Coque aux Truffes
(Boiled eggs with truffles)

Admittedly this little masterpiece will not be widely available outside a region of truffle-producing oaks, but it is so Périgourdin that I cannot exclude it.

When you are collecting truffles, place them in a terrine with some freshly laid eggs and leave for 3 or 4 days, well covered, before boiling them as usual. The little miracle is manifested when the eggs, no matter how they are cooked, are found to have absorbed the flavour of the truffles. This simple act demonstrates the subtlety and highly sophisticated sense of taste and refinement in the Périgord.

Les Tartines de Foie Gras aux Oeufs Frits
(Foie gras and fried eggs on toast)

This recipe originates from the days when foie gras was cut in slices and fried in a pan. It can be made equally well with pâté de foie gras.

Time: 30 minutes

1 egg per person	2 oz (50 g) plain flour
1 slice of foie gras per person	Salt and pepper
1 glass of dry white wine	1 thick slice of bread per person
10–12 shallots, sliced	Goose fat
1 truffle, sliced	

Cut thick slices of bread and scoop out some of the centre. Fry in goose fat both sides and keep hot.

Fry the foie gras or pâté in its own fat, turning carefully. Keep hot.

Cook the shallots in the pan in which you have just fried the pâté. Sprinkle over as much of the flour as you need to coat the shallots, and moisten with the white wine (plus a little broth or water if necessary). Add the sliced truffle. Fry the eggs both sides. Put a slice of pâté on each piece of bread, an egg on top of the pâté and pour the sauce over. Serve immediately.

Soufflé au Foie Gras
(Foie gras soufflé)

Time: 25 minutes
Serves 4–6

3 eggs, separated
8 oz (250 g) foie gras
½ pint (300 ml) single cream

1 oz (30 g) butter
Salt and pepper

Blend the foie gras, egg yolks and cream. Season with moderation. Beat the egg whites to stiff points and incorporate into the foie gras mixture. Grease a soufflé dish with the butter and pour in the soufflé mixture. Cook in a hot oven (425°F, 220°C, Gas 7) for 25 minutes. Serve at once.

Les Plats Composés
(Made-up Dishes)

Les Crispés de Montignac
(Montignac crispies)

There are few entrées so simple to prepare, so economical and so delightful as this.

Time: A few minutes
Serves 6

A heaped plateful of breadcrumbs (the plate should be
   about 9 ins (24 cms) in
   diameter

3 egg whites
2–3 tbsp walnut or olive oil
A tomato sauce (page 119)

Prepare a tomato sauce and keep warm.
   Beat the egg whites into stiff points and mix into the breadcrumbs. Heat the oil in a frying-pan. Taking spoonfuls of the mixture form it into balls and fry crisply, turning the balls so that they are evenly

browned. (The mixture swells in cooking.) Arrange on a heated dish and serve with the tomato sauce.

Les Feuilles de l'Oseille en Beignets
(Sorrel fritters)

This recipe is equally good with salsify or young globe artichokes.

Time: a few minutes
Serves 4–6

4 oz (125 g) plain flour	1 egg yolk
2–3 tbsp water	2 egg whites, beaten stiffly
1 tbsp eau-de-vie or alcohol	Sorrel leaves, 6–8 per person
Salt and pepper	Oil for frying

Make a batter with the flour, water, eau-de-vie or alcohol, salt, pepper and egg yolk. Wash the sorrel leaves and trim the stalks just long enough to be held easily. Heat the oil in the pan. When hot, incorporate the beaten egg whites into the batter and beat vigorously. The batter is now a mousse.

Dip the sorrel leaves into the mixture and give each a good coating. Drop into the hot fat, a few at a time as the batter will swell. Keep each batch drained and hot until all the beignets have been cooked. Serve sprinkled with fine salt. The fritters are very good on their own, but can be served with tiny grilled sausages or as a garnish to other dishes.

Les Surprises de Foie Gras
(Foie gras surprises)

A most exquisite and easily made entrée

Time: 20 minutes
Serves 4

4 paper cornets	Parsley and watercress to garnish
4 slices jambon de pays, York or Paris ham	2 tbsp goose fat
5 hard-boiled eggs	8 oz (250 g) foie gras or pâté de foie gras
1 truffle, sliced	A little white wine

Note: If you use jambon de pays (salted ham), soak for 30 minutes to desalt it.

Fry the thin slices of ham on both sides. Insert the slices into the paper cornets in a spiral fashion. Melt the goose fat and pour carefully down the cornets. Allow to go cold (this helps to seal the cornets). Leave them to take shape.

Make a purée by heating the foie gras in a little white wine and mashing it with the sliced truffle. Shell 4 of the eggs and mash them.

When you are sure the cornets have taken shape, put a good spoonful of the pâté purée down each. Finish filling the cornets with the mashed hard-boiled eggs and close the ends with a lid of sliced egg (the fifth egg, shelled and sliced). Insert a sprig of watercress into each 'cap'.

Arrange for serving by carefully withdrawing the paper cornets and sliding the 'surprises' onto a dish, points to the centre. Decorate with watercress or parsley.

La Queue de Beouf à la Vinaigrette
(Oxtail in vinaigrette)

This and the following recipe can be made from the meat taken off the oxtail bones when you have made *La Soupe à la Queue de Boeuf* (page 27).

Time: 5 minutes

Meat from 1 or 2 oxtails, depend-   chopped sorrel, cress and chives
ing on persons to be served (1   2 or 3 chopped shallots
oxtail serve 4 people)

For the vinaigrette
1 tbsp vinegar   Salt and pepper
3 tbsp walnut oil   1 soft-boiled egg

Take the meat from the bones while still hot and allow to go cold. Make the vinaigrette and beat in the soft-boiled egg. Chop the herbs very finely. Shred the meat (or mince it) and toss all the ingredients together in a large bowl. Season to taste.

Serve with slices of toast.

La Queue de Boeuf en Croquettes
(Oxtail croquettes)

Time: 10 minutes

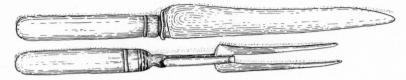

Meat from 1 or 2 oxtails, minced
2 eggs, beaten
Salt, pepper and allspice
Flour for coating

Goose fat
Tomato or onion sauce (see pages
   119 and 120)

Mix the meat, seasoning and eggs thoroughly. Form into croquettes. (A little mashed potato or breadcrumbs can be added if you don't have enough meat.) Melt the goose fat. Roll the croquettes in the flour and fry on all sides.

Serve with a tomato or onion sauce.

Les Truffes aux Four
(Roast truffles)

This is a cheat really. In fact the truffles should be cooked in cinders, but not many people have cinders available. Of course, if you do have cinders, follow the recipe up to the moment of putting the truffles in the oven and then lay them on a bed of ash in the hearth. Cover with a layer of ash and pile hot cinders on to the top layer. You will need to replace the hot cinders during the cooking time. According to gourmets, truffles cooked in cinders have the best flavour of all.

Time: 45–50 minutes

1 or 2 3–4 oz (100 g) truffles each
Streaky bacon, 1 rasher per
   truffle

Eau-de-vie or similar alcohol
Salt and pepper

Brush the truffles thoroughly and rinse under running water. Don't stand them in water as you will spoil their flavour. Pour enough eau-de-vie or similar alcohol into a bowl to give the truffles a good coating. Season with salt and pepper and wind each truffle in a rasher of streaky bacon. Wrap them in greased foil or 3 layers of greased paper. (If you are cooking them in hot cinders, wet the outer layer of paper.) Roast for 45–50 minutes in the oven (400°F, 200°C, Gas 6).

Les Truffes en Chausson
(Truffle Pasties)

A 'chausson' is puff pastry with a filling, either savoury or sweet (*chausson aux pommes*, apple pasty, for example). In appearance it is like a slightly open pasty. The previous recipe was for fresh truffles.

This recipe could be made with tinned truffles and bought puff pastry.

If you are making your own puff pastry, allow for 8–12 oz (250–375 g) flour.

Time: 15–20 minutes
Serves 6

8 oz (250 g) tinned truffles	6 tsp meat jelly (or truffle juice)
6 slices ham	Puff pastry made with 8–12 oz
6 2oz (170 g) foie gras	(250–375 g) flour

Roll out the pastry thinly and cut it into rounds of about 3'' (7 cm) diameter. Lay a slice of ham on each round of pastry, then a slice of foie gras and finish with 1 or 2 truffles. Trickle a little meat jelly or truffle juice over each. Wrap the pastry over, leaving the top open like a shoe. Cook in the oven for 15–20 minutes (450°F, 220°C, Gas 7).

La Sanguette

The nearest translation of this word would be 'a little bit of blood'. Few people will have either the possibility or the inclination to make this entrée, but it cannot be left out of this book.

Poultry here is killed by being bled into a basin because, of course, the blood must not be wasted. It would not be unreasonable to suppose that the chicken is killed for the *Sanguette*, it being so in the taste of Périgord, but in this instance the supposition would be unjust. Blood is frequently added to sauces. This recipe is yet another example of Périgordine ingenuity and invention.

I accidentally saw this dish in preparation when I arrived at a farm for some eggs as the knife was entering the neck of the chicken – I left, without eggs, before the bird was emptied.

Blood of 1 chicken	A little garlic and parsley,
Salt	chopped
A knob of goose or pork fat	

So, first bleed your bird. Have ready a pan of boiling, salted water.

Slide the blood into the water, where it immediately becomes a floppy disc. Drain the disc and dry it (imagine!). Heat a little goose or pork fat and brown the disc gently on both sides. Sprinkle with chopped garlic and parsley and serve.

Les Escargots/Les Cagouilles
(Snails)

The French think that the English live on boiled food, in particular boiled meat and potatoes. The English think that the French will eat *anything*, particularly frogs and snails. No one in my commune eats frogs, but one cold dark night I caddied for Mme Robert while she hunted snails on the walls and tombs of our cemetery. Mme Robert's knowledge and understanding of the flora and fauna of Périgord matches the Australian Aborigine's rapport with his habitat and, similarly it springs from the necessity of existing on what the woods, fields and streams have to offer. One might call it her survival kit, were it not for the wonder in her face when a speck of dust becomes an ebullient petunia, a wonder that returns every year and which marks her as a great naturalist. Colette would have appreciated Mme Robert.

Well, she knows when to hunt snails! 'They've come out to graze', she explained, raking a doomed herd with the beam of her torch. She finally gave up at the 300th snail (I shall not easily forget that pulsating tin) and they lived in a special cage until she had time to clean them – or rather, they lived in a special cage until she secretly returned them to the cemetery. This goes to show that there are French people who don't eat anything and everything. In fact, those who do eat snails eat only the snails with grey shells and only certain species of frog are eaten.

The picturesque Périgordin word in the heading of this section – '*cagouilles*' – derived from the Latin '*cagoul*' or hood. Doubtless the penitents' hood which the snail's shell resembles.

How to clean snails:

There are two principal ways of serving snails in Périgord, one with and the other without the shells. Whichever you use, the snails have to be cleaned as described below.

Mme Robert's special cage, which was no more than a box with fine mesh sides to allow the snails to breathe, can be replaced quite simply by an upturned flowerpot. Leave the snails for about 15 days under the pot to fast and then remove the whitish membrane which seals them into their shells. Put them into a basin of lukewarm water containing 2 handfuls of salt and a little vinegar. Leave them in the solution for several hours, then rinse them thoroughly in several changes of water, by which time they will be clean and ready for cooking.

How to cook snails

Time: 45 minutes

A large pan of boiling water	3 cloves
2 bay leaves	Pepper, but *very little* salt (the
A sprig each of basil and thyme	snails will have absorbed salt
A handful of black peppercorns	in the cleaning process)

Throw the snails into the boiling liquid and cook for 45 minutes. At the end of this time, test to see if they are cooked by trying to remove one or two from their shells. If they come out easily, they're cooked.

RECIPES WITH SHELLS

Les Escargots au Jus
(Snails in sauce)

Time 1½ hours
Serves 2–4 according to appetite (only 2 people in Périgord)

Note: Don't make too much sauce. There is an old saying here: 'Each snail has his own overcoat of sauce'. There should be just enough sauce to coat and soak into the shells.

The sauce: (per 2 dozen snails)

2 rashers of chopped bacon	1 good glass white wine
2 cloves garlic, crushed	Handful of spinach or chicory,
Salt, pepper	chopped
1 sprig each chervil and parsley	Stock if needed
1 egg yolk	A few finely chopped walnuts
2 tbsp walnut oil	(optional)

Put all the ingredients apart from the egg yolk and walnut oil into a pan and cook gently for 1½ hours. The liquid will reduce, so add a little stock if needed.

Having previously cleaned and cooked the snails (see above), remove them from their shells.

Wash the shells thoroughly, dry them and put the snails back into them. Add the snails to the reduced sauce and turn them about a bit to make sure they are well impregnated. At the last moment, beat the egg yolk with the walnut oil and add to the sauce. (Some cooks add finely chopped walnuts at this point.)

Les Escargots Farcis à la Périgourdine
(Stuffed snails)

This dish is particularly good grilled over a charcoal fire.

Time: 2½–3 hours
Serves 2–4 (2 in the Périgord)

6–8 pints (3–4 litres) court bouillon made from
3 onions, chopped
3 carrots, chopped
½–1 bottle good dry white wine
2 bay leaves
1 sprig of thyme (preferably wild thyme – more delicate and leaves no after-taste)
Seasoning (be lavish with the pepper but careful with the salt)

For the stuffing
3 oz (80 g) breadcrumbs
3 oz (80 g) butter
Salt and pepper
2–3 sprigs parsley, finely chopped
2 soupsp finely chopped garlic

Clean the snails as described earlier (see p.50). Bring the court bouillon to the boil and drop in the snails. Test them at the end of 45 minutes, but, apart from removing them to test, leave them in the shells; part of the pleasure of this dish is the flavour of the broth in the shells.

Pound the stuffing ingredients into a paste. Remove the snails *in* their shells from the court bouillon and keep warm. Push the stuffing into the shells on top of the snails until it is level with the opening. Place the snails on a rack under the grill and leave just long enough for the stuffing to brown and swell a little. Serve at once.

RECIPES WITHOUT SHELLS

Feuilletés d'Escargots aux Cèpes
(Snail and cèpe pasties)

Time: Allow 1½ hours to make the puff pastry, 12 minutes to cook.

12 oz (375 g) plain flour
Salt
1 lb (500 g) butter
1 pint (½ litre) tin of cèpes
1 egg
1 pint (½ litre) tin of snails
1 large/2 small cloves garlic

6 oz (170 g) shallots
Juice of 1 lemon
Small carton of fresh cream
1 glass dry white wine
4 oz (125 g) parsley
A little walnut oil.

To make the pastry, sift flour and salt. Make a hollow in the centre and pour in the water and mix rapidly. Form it into a ball and leave in a cool place for 10–15 minutes.

Work half the butter to a malleable consistency. Roll out the pastry into the shape of a cross. Flatten the butter and put it in the centre. Fold the arms of the cross on top of the butter. Roll out the pastry away from you until it is ½'' (1 cm) thick. Fold in 3 and turn through 90 degrees. Roll again and fold again. Wrap in a damp cloth and leave in the cool for 10–15 minutes.

Repeat this operation twice more.

Finally, roll out the pastry to about ¼'' (5–6 mm) and cut into squares of about 4'' (6 cm). Put on to a greased tray and cook for about 12 minutes at 450°F, 220°C, Gas 7.

Put the other half of the butter, the parsley, the garlic, the shallots, lemon juice, salt and pepper into the blender and reduce to smooth paste, then refrigerate.

Gently heat the cèpes in some walnut oil. Keep hot.

Heat the snails rapidly in the wine, mix in the fresh cream, add the refrigerated butter mixture and beat with a fork while heating. As soon as it is well-blended, withdraw from the heat. Divide the pastry slices in two, reserving one piece for a top or lid. Lay a layer of cèpes and snails on each base, pour over some sauce, put on the lids and serve at once.

Les Escargots à la Sauce Blanche
(Snails in a white sauce)

Time: 1 hour
Serves 2–4 (2 in the Périgord)

As many snails as you think
people will eat

2 rashers streaky bacon, finely
chopped

Sauce (for 12 snails):
2 tbsp walnut or olive oil
2 tbsp plain flour
1 tumbler tepid water
Salt, pepper and allspice
1 sprig parsley

1 egg yolk
Sliced gherkins to garnish
1 large/2 small onions, finely
chopped
Toast

Clean and cook the snails as described earlier (see p. 50). Remove them from their shells. Drain and dry on a clean cloth.

Mix the finely chopped onion with the walnut or olive oil. Add in the flour gradually and thin with a little water. Cook gently for 45 minutes, stirring frequently.

Brown the snails in a little walnut oil for 10 minutes. Add them to the sauce. Pound the garlic and parsley together and incorporate into the sauce. At the last moment beat the egg yolk with a little of the sauce and add to the sauce.

Serve on toast and decorate with sliced gherkins.

Les Entrées de Poisson
(Fish Entrées)

Les Ecrivisses Flambées
(Freshwater crayfish flambées)

Time: 1½ hours

Some of the streams in Périgord are very low in summer and one can walk in the water barefoot or in espadrilles, turning over the larger stones to find the crayfish. Sometimes one finds a fish under every stone! This hunt, for it could hardly be called 'fishing', can become a passion, a passion needing neither expensive equipment nor disgusting bait for its satisfaction.

As many crayfish as you need each
2 tbsp walnut or olive oil
2 glasses good white wine (at least)

1 liqueur glass cognac
2 or 3 tomatoes, skinned, seeded and quartered, or a small tin of whole tomatoes (4 oz, 125 g)
Parsley for decoration

The sauce (for about 12 crayfish)
2 good carrots, chopped
2 sticks celery, chopped
1 large/2 small onions, chopped
2–3 shallots, chopped

2 cloves garlic, chopped
Oil for browning
Salt, cayenne, allspice, parsley, thyme and a bay leaf

Prepare the crayfish by removing the bitter nodule in the centre of the tail fin. Wash the fish in several changes of water. It is customary throughout France to cook the crayfish in a court bouillon at this stage, but of course in Périgord one does differently: the crayfish are cooked with an excellent sauce.

You will need 2 pans as the fish and sauce are started off separately.

Gently brown (*doré*) the finely chopped carrot, celery, onion, shallot and garlic. Season with the herbs and spices.

Heat 2 tbsp walnut or olive oil in the other pan and cook the crayfish for a few moments. Add at least 2 glasses of wine and the brandy. Set alight (flambé) and extinguish the flames as they decline. Put in the tomatoes. Cook briskly for 10 minutes, stirring frequently. Remove from the heat.

Add a good glass of the juices in which the crayfish were cooked to the first pan. Leave the sauce to simmer for an hour. At the end of the hour, strain the sauce into the pan with the crayfish. Continue cooking for a further 15 minutes.

Serve on a heated dish with the sauce poured over the fish. Decorate with sprigs of parsley.

Le Pain de Saumon
(Salmon mousse)

This recipe is a useful way of using the remains of a whole salmon. It can also be made with tinned salmon.

Traditionally, the mousse would be cooked in the hot ashes with cinders piled on the lid.

Time: ¾–1 hour
Serves 4

The flesh remaining on a cooked salmon and/or 1 tin of salmon (total weight: 1 lb (500 g)) 3 eggs, separated	A little broth or milk Salt, cayenne (or allspice) Parsley and chervil 2–3 oz (50–80 g) breadcrumbs

Remove the meat from the salmon, taking care to avoid any bones and skin. Moisten the breadcrumbs with a little broth or milk and beat in the salmon. Chop the parsley and chervil finely and beat in the egg yolks. Season with salt and cayenne (or allspice if preferred) and incorporate into the salmon mixture. Beat the egg whites to a stiff consistency and fork briskly into the salmon mixture.

Grease a mould and put in the salmon mousse. Stand the mould in a dish of water and cook for ¾–1 hour at 350°F, 180°C, Gas 4.

To serve hot: Remove the mousse carefully from the mould. Place on a hot dish and serve with tomato sauce (see page 119).

To serve cold: Put the mousse on a platter and decorate with rounds of hard-boiled egg and gherkins, and serve with a vinaigrette or verjuice.

La Truite aux Truffes de Monseigneur
(Truffle-stuffed trout for the bishop)

There is no record of who made this dish for which lucky bishop.

Note: It is usual to stuff large trout. The amount of stuffing given is *per trout*. The number of truffles used must be decided by the purse and taste of the cook, and, obviously, the quantity of the stuffing depends on the size of the fish.

Time: Since trout take only 5–8 minutes a side to cook, the stuffing should be made in advance and kept in a cool place. 15 minutes to cook.

The stuffing
The original list of ingredients I was given for this stuffing included *'un blanc de poulet'* – one chicken breast, but, typical of the Périgordines, the age and weight of the chicken was not made clear. The Périgordins would not call this 'guess-work', they would *know* at a glance how much *blanc de poulet* each trout would require, and, confident that other cooks can do as well, I have listed the ingredients as they were given to me.

1 truffle	1 glass white wine
1 cooked breast of chicken, minced	A knob of butter
1 tbsp grillons de Périgord (see page 114)	A handful of pickled nasturtium seeds (see page 148)
Salt and pepper	A little lemon juice or verjuice

Simmer the truffle in the wine for 8–10 minutes. Do *not* allow to boil. Remove from the wine and slice finely. (If you find it easier to slice the truffle raw, no harm will come to the flavour by cooking the slices rather than the whole truffle.)

Mix the chicken and grillons, add the truffle and season with salt, pepper and a few nasturtium seeds. Blend together with the butter.

Slit the belly of the trout, clean it, wash it and descale it. Make a couple of incisions each side. Insert the stuffing, wrap the fish in greased paper or foil and cook under a hot grill for 5–8 minutes each side, depending on the size of the fish. Serve immediately with lemon juice or verjuice trickled over.

Friture Périgourdine
(Périgord fish fry)

8 oz (250 g) small trout, gudgeon and/or gardêche (minnow)
A persilade of crushed garlic and

parsley and finely chopped walnuts

A quick, refreshing fish entrée.

Deep fry trout, gudgeon or gardêche. Drain and serve with a 'persilade' (crushed garlic and parsley and finely chopped walnuts).

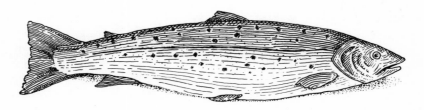

Les Pâtés

I am often asked why I have come here to live, a question followed unfailingly by where do I want to be buried; so far, I have not found a definitive answer to either question. On a practical level, I am going to *have* to solve the second, but I doubt whether I shall ever understand the forces which brought me to this tiny village, more than 1,000 miles from my birthplace in Yorkshire.

In fact, Yorkshire and this particular part of Périgord have much in common. The rolling hills, the softness of the colours, the loose stone walls and the ancient houses and churches that seem to have grown naturally too, could be transplanted without either Yorkshire or Périgord rejecting the foreign bodies. The weather is the principal difference. It is the weather and the five rivers of Périgord that give the region its abundance and variety; and that difference between the two places makes one particular facet of both all the more surprising. Both Yorkshire and le Périgord are famous for their potted meats.

The term 'potted meat' covers all methods of conserving meat, whether it be a confit de canard, a pâté or a simple conserve of pork. The extreme winters in the Yorkshire hills made potted meat a life-saving necessity in the old days, and even today bad weather can cut off the deep freezer and access to fresh food. Why the women of Périgord have perfected all forms of food conservation is hard to divine, but perfect it they have. Le Périgord is the country of the home conserve par excellence: fruit, vegetables, mushrooms, meat, ready-cooked dishes – all are put into tins and jars, hermetically sealed and sterilized. No Périgordin housewife is caught off-guard: she has cupboards, *storerooms*, full of every imaginable delicacy, and can produce a complete meal (by which I mean six courses) in a very short time. Everything is scrupulously labelled, and my own larder has several gifts such as 'Haricots Verts 1981' and 'Les Rosées (a delicious mushroom) 1983' from the kitchens of Mme Robert, one of our most prolific and successful conservers.

Home-tinning has been possible in Périgord since before the Second World War. During that war, the Périgordins sent litre tins of eau-de-vie to their men in prisoner-of-war camps – doubtless labelled 'Tourin Blanchi' – and at that time the lids were soldered on. Nowadays, most communes have a machine for sealing tins and in our village it is the grocer who both sells the tins and has the machine, a machine which can be adjusted to accommodate different sizes of tin. One buys a dozen or more assorted tins, goes home to fill them with pâté, confit or French beans, returns to the grocer to have the lids sealed in place, and – if you haven't a big enough sterilizer at home – the grocer's wife will sterilize them for you (price added to cost per tin, naturally).

We are still in '*Les Entrées*' of course, and there is no better entrée to begin a meal with than that pâte for which the Périgordins are so justly renowned: the *Pâté de Foie Gras au Truffe*.

Pâté de Foie Gras de Canard ou d'Oie au Truffe
(Duck or goose liver pâté with truffle)

Making pâté de foie gras is *very* easy. Making the liver fat is not. Maize is still the grain used in force-feeding, and the goose will be forced to feed when it isn't hungry. The birds are put into a special wooden box with a hole in the top for the head to poke through. The person administering the grain sits on the box and takes hold of the goose by the neck. There are various methods for getting the maize into the goose (one local woman uses a mouli), the most usual being a wide-necked funnel down which handfuls of grain are pushed with a wooden spoon or by a special gadget attached to the funnel. From time to time, the bird's neck is massaged from head to chest to help the grain on its way. It is said that the goose gets a sense of security from these 'caresses'. I make no attempt to force-feed you this grain of hypocrisy. Each bird is given about 1½ kilos of maize daily. Fortunately for the geese, they are only force-fed for the last four to five weeks of their lives, and a keen watch is kept on their weight to avoid sudden death by apoplexy before the liver has reached the required proportions. Immediately after they are killed, the birds are hung by their feet to be drained of their blood. (It is at this season that 'la Sanguette' is enjoyed on the tables of Pèrigord, page 49.)

Note for the curious: birds cannot be sick.

The history of 'gavage' (force-feeding) began before the Jews were driven out of Egypt. There are frescos suggesting that force-feeding was known at that time, and it is generally thought that it was the Jews who brought the secret out of Egypt and finally into Europe. I say 'the secret', because this is how the process is seen by gastronomic enthusiasts, but one cannot avoid a comparison, a liaison even, with Charles Lamb's essays on the origins of roast pork: origins, to his mind, rooted in accident. A sty catches fire, the pork's owner, sadly touching the charred corpse, burns his fingers and licks them to soothe the blister – voilà! Wild geese come down from long flights to graze. They feed abundantly, stocking energy for the next long haul. Someone kills and eats a bird and finds the enlarged liver particularly tasty – et voilà! But either it didn't happen like that, or the 'someone' kept his secret, for foie gras has not always been so generally produced.

The exact moment when force-feeding began in Périgord is not known. Some say that 'the secret' was jealously guarded by the Jews in Alsace until this century, but earlier reference to force-feeding make this theory untenable. Rabelais, for instance, tells of a monk who swears by the 'saint of fattening geese'. P. Belou, a naturalist in the reign of François I, speaks of it and, at the end of the sixteenth century, Charles Étienne and J. Libault gave 'forceful' details of the steps to take to obtain fattened livers. The possible moment of its introduction into Périgord was in the eighteenth century, when maize coming over the Pyrennees into south-west France became the common denominator in the feeding of man and poultry alike. Maize became the providential grain to supplement other sources of flour (see *La Mique*, page 26), the grain that helped men through the sporadic famines that still devastated certain areas of the south-west. It was maize that brought about the great production of foie gras in Périgord and which from that moment gained its reputation. It was at *that* moment that terrines and pâtés of foie gras were sent to the courts of Europe by special couriers, since when they have become celebrated throughout the world. Why is this?

The instant acclaim for the pâtés and terrines of Périgord, and the reasons for the continuing dominance of their reputation over those of Normandy and Alsace, may be explained partly, perhaps, by the benefits of the Périgord's geographic situation and consequent quality of produce, and partly by the importance of the pig in the life of the Périgordins. The Jews of Alsace would not have mixed pork meat with their foie gras, for instance, and it is this blend of meats, not to mention the truffle that grows in Périgord, which has given the pâtés and terrines of this area their unique flavour. It is true that making *Pâté de Foie Gras au Truffe* is easy. All you need are *good ingredients* and the *proper balance* of meats.

Time: 2½ hours or 30 minutes to sterilize

For each tin/jar you will need:

4 oz (125 g) duck or goose liver	Salt and pepper
4 oz (125g) breast of pork	A little cognac
2 thin slices truffle	

Mince the pork. Season and moisten with a few drops of cognac. Mix thoroughly. Cut the red veins from the duck or goose liver and weigh out portions of 4 oz (125 g). Lay a slice of truffle in the bottom of a tin or kilner jar. Put 2 oz (50 g) minced pork in the container, then 4 oz (125 g) liver and finished with a second 2 oz (50 g) of minced pork. Place another slice of truffle on top. A little salt may be sprinkled over the liver but usually there is enough salt in the pork to season the pâté. Seal the tins or jars hermetically and sterilize for 2½ hours by conventional means or 30 minutes in a pressure cooker. Turn the tins or jars upside-down to cool, to equalize the fat.

This pâté improves with age.

Note: Always put the tins or jars in the refrigerator for a couple of hours before opening. This solidifies the fat so that it can be removed and put aside for reuse.

Terrine de Foie Gras d'Oie au Truffe
(Potted goose liver with truffle)

The inclusion of this recipe demonstrates consistency in my approach to life. Richardson's *Clarissa*, Gilbert White's *Natural History of Selborne* and the works of Jorge Luis Borges may never be asked for from the public library, but they should be on the shelves. As with many terrines, this one should be made several days before it is to be used, so that the truffle can 'perfume' the dish.

Time: 1¼–1½ hours

1 goose's liver	2 oz (50 g) streaky bacon
2 truffles	4 oz (125 g) minced lean pork
3 tbsp eau-de-vie or similar	Salt and pepper
alcohol	Flour-and-water paste
Goose fat	

Choose a liver that is a good pink in colour and firm to touch. Leave it to soak in water overnight. Next day, drain and dry on a clean cloth.

Make some incisions in the liver one inch apart. Brush and wash the truffles carefully, peel and slice them. Insert a slice of truffle into each of the incisions made in the liver.

Cover the bottom of a terrine with thinly sliced rashers of streaky bacon. Put the whole goose liver on top of the bacon. Fill in any gaps round the liver with minced pork. Season with salt and pepper and sprinkle the eau-de-vie over the liver. Melt enough goose fat to cover the whole surface. Line the edge of the lid and the rim of the terrine with a stiff flour-and-water paste to seal it.

Stand the terrine in a dish of water and cook in a moderate oven (350°F, 180°C, Gas 4) for 1¼–1½ hours.

Stand the terrine in a cool place for 2–3 days before using.

If you want to serve the pâté out of the terrine, stand it in boiling water for a few minutes, turn upside-down over a clean platter and gently ease out the pâté. Remove the excess fat and the bacon, and garnish with parsley or watercress.

Terrine de Foie de Canard
(Potted duck liver)

Time: Actual cooking time 40 minutes, but allow 24 hours to complete this recipe.

2 duck livers weighing 1¼ lb (600 g) each	1 thin rasher streaky bacon
2 pt (1 l) milk	8 fl.oz (250 ml) Armagnac
	Salt, pepper and a little nutmeg

Pull out the principal veins from the livers and leave the livers to soak in just enough milk to cover for 2 hours. Drain and dry. Season with salt, pepper and a little nutmeg. Place in a terrine and pour over the Armagnac. Leave in a cool place for at least 12 hours, turning the livers occasionally to take up the alcohol.

To cook: lift out the livers, put the streaky bacon into the bottom of the terrine. Replace the livers, cover with foil and stand the terrine in a dish of water. Cook in a medium oven (375°F, 190°C, Gas 5) for 40 minutes. Keep an eye on the liver towards the end of the cooking time as they should remain slightly pink. Remove excess fat and reserve. Allow the livers to go cold. Remove the bacon and replace the livers in the terrine. Melt the fat you drained off and pour over. Put the livers in cool place until ready for use.

Pâté de Foie de Porc
(Pork liver pâté)

Time: 2 hours

3 lb (1.5 kg) pork liver
2 lb (1 kg) breast of pork
1 lb (500 g) fresh lard
2 eggs, beaten

1 soupsp flour
Salt, pepper and a little allspice
A piece of larding bacon
Flour-and-water paste

Heat oven to 350°F, 180°C, Gas 4.

Cut out the hard membrane at the interior of the liver. Mince the pork breast, the liver and the lard together finely. Add the flour, the eggs, salt, pepper and allspice, and make sure the ingredients are well-blended.

Spread a layer of the pâté on the bottom of a large terrine and put some well-seasoned larding strips on top. Continue adding alternate layers of pâté and larding, ending with a layer of pâté. Cover carefully, sealing the lid to the rim of the terrine with a stiff paste of flour and water to ensure that the pâte remains absolutely closed during cooking. Place the terrine in a dish of water in the oven and cook at moderate heat for 2 hours.

Leave at least 48 hours before cutting into the pâté.

Le Pâté de Campagne
(Country pâté)

Time: 3 hours

This pâté keeps well.

The eau-de-vie in this recipe may be replaced by any alcohol (50 degrees) available, but it is advisable to choose one with the least strong flavour .

3 lb (1.5 kg) lean pork
1 lb (500 g) breast of pork
   (streaky)
12 oz (375 g) veal or ham
1 lb (500 g) fresh lard
1 lb (500 g) onions, chopped
1 small glass eau-de-vie

Chopped parsley
1 tsp allspice
½ oz (15 g) fine salt
A good pinch of pepper
3 rashers streaky larding
Flour-and-water paste

Mince together the pork, the streaky joint, the veal or ham, the onions and the lard, and work in the seasoning, herbs, allspice and alcohol.

Put the pâté into a large terrine and cover with streaky lardings. Cover and seal the lid to the rim of the terrine with a little stiff flour-and-water paste. Stand in a dish of water in the oven and cook for 3 hours at medium heat. Leave to get quite cold before using.

Le Pâté de Lapin ou de Lièvre
(Rabbit or hare pâté)

Since myxomatosis raged through the rabbit communities of Europe, many people are chary of eating rabbit. From mid-September though, the Périgord resounds with the throaty baying of man and dog and the sharp fusillades of shotguns. Of course, nobody eats a diseased animal, but since everyone in the country rears rabbits for home consumption, this pâté is to be found throughout the region. Inevitably, the flavour is not as good when tame rabbit is used.

Mme Robert, our mushroom queen, gave me this recipe. It is extremely good. Her advice is to leave it for four or five days before eating as it improves in flavour with keeping. She also told me not to remove the lid until the pâté was completely cold. Mme Robert's husband is (I quote) 'clever' with his car wheels: hardly a week passes without him bringing home a rabbit or hare that has run into his headlights in the early hours of the morning.

Time: 2 hours

2 lb (1 kg) rabbit meat	A good pinch pepper
12 oz (375 g) veal	A good pinch of nutmeg
12 oz (375 g) fat bacon	A good pinch of allspice
6 oz (170 g) streaky bacon	2 soupsp eau-de-vie
1 oz (30 g) fine salt	1 good piece of larding
1 carrot	1 bouquet garni
1 large onion	Flour-and-water paste

Bone the rabbit. Put the bones, the rind from the bacon, 1 carrot, 1 large onion cut in pieces, salt, pepper and bouquet garni in a pan. Cover with water and cook gently until the liquid is reduced to about half. Strain.

Choose about 20 good pieces of rabbit meat and veal meat and leave them whole. Mince all the rest, along with the fat and streaky bacon. Season. Add the eau-de-vie and mix well with a wooden spoon, gradually adding the strained liquid from the bones. Put a piece of larding into the bottom of a pâté terrine, then spread a layer of the pâté in the terrine, then some pieces of whole rabbit and veal, then another layer of pâté and so on, finishing with a layer of pâté.

Put a piece of larding on top, cover and seal the lid to the edge of the terrine with a stiff flour-and-water paste. Place in a dish of water and cook in a moderate oven for 2 hours.

Le Pâté de Faisan aux Truffes
(Pheasant pâté with truffles)

Time: 2 hours

This same recipe can be used for all game-birds such as partridges, woodcocks and larks.

1¼ lb (600 g) pheasant meat	1 oz (30 g) salt
7 oz (200 g) veal	A good pinch of pepper and
1 lb (500 g) fat larding	allspice
1 truffle	2 egg yolks
2 tbsp Cognac	Flour-and-water paste

Bone the pheasant completely when freshly killed. Put the pieces of breast into a bowl to soak in some Cognac and turn them from time to time.

Mince all the meats and larding (except for the breasts soaking in Cognac) finely. Season with salt, pepper and allspice, and bind with the beaten egg yolks. Put a layer of the pâté in an oval terrine, lay the whole pieces of Cognac-impregnated breasts over it and finish with another layer of pâté. Slice a truffle in rounds and arrange on top. Line the lid and edge of the terrine with a stiff flour-and-water paste and cook in a dish of water in a moderate oven for 2 hours.

This pâté is best left for at least 48 hours before removing the lid, and will keep for 10 days if not cut into and stored in a cool place.

This section will be of particular interest to the freshwater fisherman. Though Périgord has contact with Bordeaux and its seafoods, five major rivers and hundreds of streams and lakes producing delicious freshwater fish have stimulated the Périgordines to perfect the cooking of inland water fish so that their delicate flavour is never lost. To a town-dweller, these recipes may seem unrealistic, but I include them for the benefit of those enthusiasts to whom fresh-caught river fish are available. The growth of trout-farming makes that particular fish easily procurable, of course.

Mme Robert, an excellent fish cook, gave me the following tips (or '*tuyaux*', since we are in the world of Périgord). The first tuyau is that trout bought the day before you wish to cook them won't curl in the cooking. The second deals with the serving of verjuice or lemon juice. Mme Robert never serves fish in the juices it has been cooked in, unless, of course, the juices are an integral part of a sauce. Her advice is to lift the fish out of the juices and keep it hot, and in a fresh pan melt a little butter, to which is added the juice of a lemon and a clove of garlic crushed with some parsley. Leave this for a minute for the ingredients or take on one another's flavours before pouring out over the fish.

The term 'court bouillon' appears in many fish recipes. It means a liquid of wine, herbs and spices in which fish are cooked.

Les Truites Grillées sur la Braise
(Trout grilled over a fire)

If you have an open fire, particularly a wood-burning fire, this recipe will give you a meal to remember. If not, it can be grilled or barbecued, but not fried!

Time: 10 minutes

1 trout per person
ground juniper berries to coat
    fish (1 tbsp per trout)

Clean and wash the fish. Dip the trout in ground juniper berries giving both sides a good coating. Place them on a gridiron and cook

over hot ashes for 5 minutes each side.
    This is exquisite!

Les Truites à Vinaigre à la Sauce de Vin Blanc
(Trout cooked in vinegar with white wine sauce)

Time 30 minutes

White wine sauce (page 118)   A little parsley
1 trout per person   ½ pint (300 ml) wine vinegar

Clean and bone the fish. If you find boning difficult try this method.
Cut off the head. Make an incision along the belly. Turn the fish spine
uppermost and open out the belly from side to side. Put your thumb
on the trout's back and, starting at the head end, press firmly down
along the length of the spine to the tail. Turn the fish over. Put a knife
under the spine at the head end to raise it so you can take hold of it
firmly. Pull away the spine from the flesh – it should come out intact,
smaller bones and all.
    Have ready a shallow pan of boiling wine vinegar and water. Dip
the fish in undiluted wine vinegar and plunge into the boiling pan.
Allow to poach for 10 minutes, drain, arrange on a heated dish, pour
over the white wine sauce and garnish with parsley.

Le Brochet à la Broche
(Pike cooked on a wooden spit)

Pike abound in Périgord and it is a wonder that other species survive.
It is known as the 'freshwater shark', devouring not only fish smaller
than itself but fish of its own race – even its young. Mrs Beeton
describes the flesh as 'rather dry', but since there are said to be fifty
ways of cooking the monster in Périgord, one must suppose the
Périgordins think more highly of it than she did. They think very
highly indeed of its liver, which is seen as a great delicacy.
    M. Tonneau has pike in his pond, and when he is interested in
doing someone a favour he gives them leave to fish his waters. I was
once invited to take Sunday lunch with the family – to celebrate the
publication of one of my books with one of *my* bottles of champagne,
the end of a good meal in good company being the proper place for
champagne, according to M. Tonneau. We had almost reached that
stage of the meal when his bank manager entered bearing a pike, it
being the custom to give a part of your catch to the owner of the
waters. Other than an awe-inspiring illustration in my original 'Mrs
Beeton' of a pike peering balefully through engraved fronds of

pondweed, I had never seen a pike. Neither had M. Tonneau's grandchildren. They jostled one another to stroke the fish, though his seven-year-old granddaughter said she didn't like the look of its teeth. There were other things I didn't like about the pike, things that made me wonder if M. Tonneau, who identifies powerfully with Napoleon, had not met his Waterloo in his bank manager: the fish might well have come out of his pond, but *when*?

There were nine people round that table, not counting the children, and eight of the fifty available recipes were put forward for cooking the pike. (No one expected the English woman to know a recipe.) The bank manager was scarcely over the threshold, when our host took a measure from the pocket of his Sunday jacket to check the pike's length. 'Fifty centimetres', he muttered, allowing the measure to snap into its case. 'He should have thrown it back.'

Even to townsfolk, 50 cms from snout to tail is not very big for a pike, particularly since it is a slim fish, a fact that should be taken into account when calculating the portions to be served. For recipes without a stuffing, a 5 lb (2.5 kg) pike should serve 6 people. For recipes with a stuffing, 4 lb (2 kg) should suffice for the same number.

The following recipe is one of the best of the fifty mentioned, both because it is nowadays an unusual way of cooking and because, for some reason, pike is better when treated like poultry. The ideal method is before an open fire, but life isn't perfect and failing the ideal, you can make use of your oven. In any case, you will need a wooden spit arranged over a dripping-pan to catch the basting juices. Ovens are often supplied with spits these days, but fish is better cooked on a wooden rather than a metal spit.

Time: 45 minutes
Serves 6

1 pike of 5 lb (2.5 kg)
Salt and cayenne pepper
Enough larding to spike the fish
½ bottle dry white wine
2 egg yolks

2–3 shallots, sliced
1 tbsp walnut oil or butter
A handful of pickled nasturtium
seeds (see p. 148)

Even if your pike comes direct from a lake or pond it will probably be dead by the time it lies on your kitchen table; but dead or alive, you will have to clean and scale it – a procedure that will kill it if it is alive.

To kill, scale and clean pike
Follow this procedure whether you are dealing with a dead or just killed fish. The hot water makes scaling easy.

You will need a receptacle large enough to take the fish and enough water to cover it well. Raise the heat of the water to the point where you can no longer keep your finger in it. Throw in the fish and slam on a lid to prevent the tail from thrashing about. The fish will be dead in a matter of seconds. Remove it from the hot water and scale it with a sharp knife. Plunge the fish into cold water to firm the flesh. Make an incision in the belly, clean the fish and dry thoroughly.

Keep the liver (dark red) but do *not* use the roe (white to orange), it is *poisonous*.

To cook

Spike the body of the pike with lardings and arrange on the wooden spit over a dripping-pan either before a hot fire or in a brisk oven (425–50°F, 220–30°C, Gas 7–8). Season with salt and cayenne pepper. Pour over the dry white wine and cook for 45 minutes, turning and basting frequently.

Towards the end of the cooking make the sauce. Warm the walnut oil or butter in a pan and gently cook the sliced shallots, adding in one or two spoonfuls of the basting juices. At the last moment, thicken the sauce with the beaten egg yolks, throw in a handful of pickled nasturtium seeds and serve with (but not poured over) the fish.

The liver:

The pike's liver may be cooked gently in walnut or olive oil and served with a sauce of verjuice or lemon juice and pounded garlic and parsley.

La Carpe Farcie aux cèpes
(Carp with cèpe stuffing)

Time: Allow 1 hour for a fish of 6 lb (3 kg)
Serves 8

1 6 lb (3 kg) carp
Salt, pepper and a pinch of
   allspice

For the stuffing:
14 oz (400 g) grillons (page 114)
4 oz (125 g) salt bacon
3 shallots, finely chopped
4 oz (125 g) cèpe or small tin of
   cèpes
bouquet garni (parsley, thyme
   and basil sprigs)
2 large cloves garlic, chopped
1 egg, beaten with 1 tbsp eau-de-
   vie or alcohol at 45° with no
   flavour
4 oz (125 g) breadcrumbs

For the sauce:

2 glasses dry white wine

1 tbsp walnut or olive oil

1 carrot, finely chopped

1 onion, finely chopped

2 egg yolks

Scale and clean the carp as explained on p.68 for the pike. Wash and dry throughly. Season.

Mince the bacon. Mix together all the stuffing ingredients and bind with the beaten egg and eau-de-vie or alcohol. Push the stuffing into the belly of the carp and tie with string, taking care not to damage the flesh. Place the fish in an ovenproof dish, arrange the chopped carrot and onion round it, trickle the walnut or olive oil over the fish and pour on the two glasses of wine. Cook at 350°F, 180°C, Gas 4 at least 2 hours, basting regularly.

When the carp is cooked, lift on to a clean hot dish and keep warm. Sieve the juices from the ovenproof dish, thicken with two beaten egg yolks and serve with – but not over – the carp.

Note: some people make the stuffing with pâté de foie gras, truffle and brandy, but such richness is seen as pretension locally: pâté-de-foie-gras-with everything shows a lack of refinement.

L'Anguille au Vin Rouge
(Eel in red wine)

It will be a surprise to many people to find fish and red wine together, but there are several classic French recipes that marry unexpected wines and ingredients, and one may even be served a chilled red wine with a fish course (though not in this commune: that, too, would be seen as pretension). The high reputation of this dish in Périgord and south-west France is due to the quality of the red wine used in its preparation. The *unbreakable rule* for this dish is that you do *not allow* yourself to use a cheap red wine, even if it is of 8° or 10°. The alcoholic content must be high enough for the wine to be flambé (set alight), but the alcoholic content of the wine is not the measure of its quality: the wine you use must have a fine bouquet. Choose a red Bordeaux recommended to you by a reputable wine merchant, or one that you know from experience to be good.

At my first encounter with this marriage of eel and red wine the banns were read out by one of our local fishermen – a 6-litres-of-vin-du-pays-a-day man, whose fish is always in red wine, and I quote: 'When you've killed him by hitting his head against a wall, and when you've drained him of his blood into a bowl, you make a cut right round his body just under his head, and you turn back his skin, like a fine lady's glove, and, holding a cloth so that your hands won't slip on him, you pull off his skin. And you open his belly and clean him out – and you give his entrails to me for my cat.'

It is no good being squeamish about these things. Animals are reared and slaughtered in order that man may eat, but we have lost touch with the processes that bring a lamb chop to our plate.

'I thought of you in the night,' said M. Tonneau romantically one day, 'as I lay awake so as not to miss the abattoir van.'

'The *abattoir* van!'

'Don't you ever think about what happens to the condemned man in your "romans policier"?'

Well, I don't, and in any case the death penalty has been abolished. M. Tonneau is a businessman, raising calves in the dark so that their flesh will be paler. Those calves never see the light of day from birth to the arrival of the abattoir van. My open condemnation of his methods has been parried with the philosophical comment that man is in no position to assess the expectations of a beast. Cattle progress along a corridor just wide enough for them to pass on their way to death, and even though a bull has but the length of the cow in front between himself and death he will mount the cow. Animals are very sensitive to the smell of blood and death, and it is extraordinary that the urge to procreate is stronger than the instinct to fear death.

I think I am in a position to assess the expectations of an eel flung against a wall. It would not expect to be. But it is a more humane method of killing the fish than others I have had recommended to me. Mme Robert's mother was a cook in a Bordeaux wine château before the war and her method was to wrap the eel in a rough towel and strike the head one strong, dry blow on the edge of the table. 'It doesn't do to hesitate,' Mme Robert explained, 'because the eel winds itself round your arm.'

If, after all this, you still feel inclined – or even *able* – to cook eels in red wine, I suggest you buy your eels from the fishmonger and get him to kill and skin them.

Time: 1–1½ hours
Serves 4–6

2 eels of 14–16 oz (400–500 g) each
1 bottle good red wine
8 oz (250 g) streaky bacon
12 small white onions, peeled
2 large cloves of garlic, sliced
2 or 3 shallots, sliced

4 oz (125 g) cèpes (or small tin)
Salt, pepper and a little cayenne
A pinch of allspice
Eels' blood, if you have killed your own
Bouquet garni (thyme, bay leaf, parsley and fennel)

Walnut oil or goose fat
2 tbsp plain flour
A little tepid water
Garnish: slices of bread rubbed
with garlic and toasted or fried
3 hard-boiled eggs, sliced and
fried in goose fat.

Your eels being dead and skinned, cut them into chunks and stand in cold water. Melt the walnut oil or goose fat and gently fry the dozen or so small white onions to a golden colour (approximately 20–30 minutes).

Chop the bacon into small pieces and put into a flame-proof casserole with the large, sliced shallots, all the seasoning and the bouquet garni. Cover and cook *very* gently for 20 minutes.

This is the moment to select your wine. Empty the bottle of your choice into a pan and set it alight. When the flames have died down, pour the wine into the casserole with the bacon and shallots and add the little white onions to it. Cover and simmer for 15 minutes.

Blend the flour with a little tepid water (the only water permitted to enter this recipe) and add to the casserole, stirring it about a little. Cover and continue to simmer for 30 minutes.

Drain the eel pieces, dry thoroughly, and add to the casserole. Cover again. Gently heat the sliced cèpe in a little walnut oil. Add to the casserole. At the end of 30 minutes the eel should be à point (perfectly cooked). This is the moment for adding the eel's blood, should you have followed my fisherman's instructions. Mix the blood with a little of the sauce and incorporate with the rest of the contents of the casserole. *On no account should the blood boil* – but it must get hotter than your own may be at the thought. Pull the casserole off the direct flame, therefore, but keep hot.

To serve: Arrange the eel pieces in the form of a crown on a heated dish. Scoop the cèpes and onions from the pan and put in the centre of the crown. Arrange the toast around the edge of the platter with the slices of egg on top. Put one or two tablespoonsful of the sauce over the crown, and serve the rest in a sauce boat. To be truly Périgordin pour all the sauce over the eels, which makes the toast soggy of course.

Le Saumon Entier aux Ecrivisses
(Whole salmon with freshwater crayfish)

This is an impressive dish for special occasions.

Time: 1 hour
Serves 6–8

1 8 lb (4 kg) salmon, whole
12 or 18 crayfish, depending on
    size
12 small white onions, chopped
6 small carrots, chopped

Bouquet garni (thyme, parsley,
    bayleaf, fennel)
Salt and pepper
1½ bottle good dry white wine

For the sauce

1 onion, chopped
2 tbsp plain flour
Walnut oil
4 oz (125 g) cèpes (or small tin)

1 liqueur glass eau-de-vie or
    similar alcohol
1 large clove garlic, crushed with
    2 sprigs parsley
A trickle of verjuice or vinegar

Scale the salmon carefully. Clean out the entrails by the smallest possible incision. Tie the jaws together.

Pull the bitter nodule from the centre of the crayfish tails.

Lay the salmon in a long fish casserole, put in the small white onions, the carrots, the bouquet garni and the crayfish. Season and pour over a bottle of dry white wine. Bring to the boil and, as soon as the wine is boiling, reduce flame so that the liquid scarcely simmers. (If you cook on an Aga or a similar hot plate, draw the fish-cooker aside and allow to continue cooking very, very gently.) At the end of an hour the salmon should be à point.

Meanwhile, occupy yourself with the sauce. Toss the large, sliced onion in the flour. Gradually moisten with a little of the court bouillon from the fish pan. Pour half a bottle of good white wine into a casserole, add the glass of eau-de-vie and set alight. When the flames die away, blend the wine with the flour-and-onion mixture and leave to cook VERY GENTLY for 1 hour.

Remove the crayfish from the fish pan, leaving the salmon to go on cooking. Drain the crayfish on a clean cloth. Heat the walnut oil in a pan and gently fry the cèpes. Toss in the garlic and parsley and add a trickle of verjuice or vinegar. Keep warm.

To serve: strain or sieve the sauce. Drain the salmon and arrange on a long platter. Cut and remove the string round the jaws. Decorate the platter with alternate cèpes and crayfish. Serve the sauce separately, in a sauce boat.

Grilling Fish à la Périgourdine

Almost all freshwater fish are delicious grilled. In Périgord it is customary, after cleaning and washing the fish, to season them inside with salt, pepper and allspice. The fish are then sprinkled with chopped garlic and parsley and wrapped individually in oiled paper or oiled metal foil. They are cooked under the grill for about 10 minutes, and turned halfway through the cooking. They are then unwrapped and served at once, with verjuice or lemon juice dribbled over them.

LES VIANDES
— Meats —

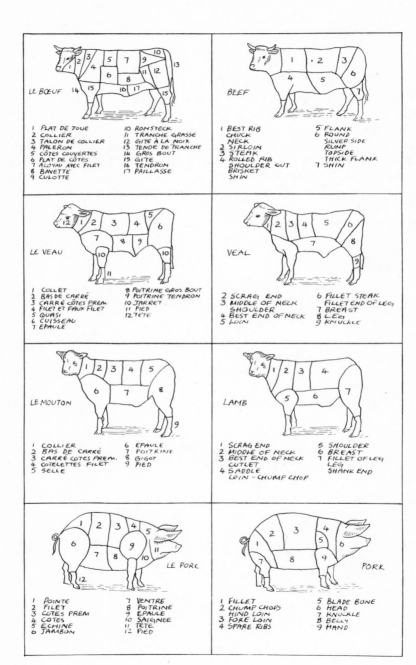

LE BŒUF

1 PLAT DE JOUE
2 COLLIER
3 TALON DE COLLIER
4 PALERON
5 CÔTES COUVERTES
6 PLAT DE CÔTES
7 ALOYAU AVEC FILET
8 BAVETTE
9 CULOTTE
10 ROMSTECK
11 TRANCHE GRASSE
12 GITE À LA NOIX
13 TENDE DE TRANCHE
14 GROS BOUT
15 GITE
16 TENDRON
17 PAILLASSE

BEEF

1 BEST RIB
  CHUCK
  NECK
2 SIRLOIN
3 STEAK
4 ROLLED RIB
  SHOULDER CUT
  BRISKET
  SHIN
5 FLANK
6 ROUND
  SILVER SIDE
  RUMP
  TOPSIDE
  THICK FLANK
7 SHIN

LE VEAU

1 COLLET
2 BAS DE CARRÉ
3 CARRÉ CÔTES PREM.
4 FILET ET FAUX FILET
5 QUASI
6 CUISSEAU
7 EPAULE
8 POITRINE GROS BOUT
9 POITRINE TENDRON
10 JARRET
11 PIED
12 TETE

VEAL

2 SCRAG END
3 MIDDLE OF NECK
  SHOULDER
4 BEST END OF NECK
5 LOIN
6 FILLET STEAK
  FILLET END OF LEG
7 BREAST
8 LEG
9 KNUCKLE

LE MOUTON

1 COLLIER
2 BAS DE CARRÉ
3 CARRÉ CÔTES PREM.
4 CÔTELETTES FILET
5 SELLE
6 EPAULE
7 POITRINE
8 GIGOT
9 PIED

LAMB

1 SCRAG END
2 MIDDLE OF NECK
3 BEST END OF NECK
  CUTLET
4 SADDLE
  LOIN - CHUMP CHOP
5 SHOULDER
6 BREAST
7 FILLET OF LEG
  LEG
  SHANK END

LE PORC

1 POINTE
2 FILET
3 CÔTES PREM
4 CÔTES
5 ECHINE
6 JAMBON
7 VENTRE
8 POITRINE
9 EPAULE
10 SAIGNEE
11 TETE
12 PIED

PORK

1 FILLET
2 CHUMP CHOPS
  HIND LOIN
3 FORE LOIN
4 SPARE RIBS
5 BLADE BONE
6 HEAD
7 KNUCKLE
8 BELLY
9 HAND

Comprising:
Le Boeuf (**Beef**)
Le Veau (**Veal**)
Le Moûton (**Mutton and Lamb**)
Le Cochon (**Pork**)
Le Gibier (**Game**)
Les Volailles (**Poultry**)
Les Confits (**Potted Meats**)

Note: It will be seen from the diagram opposite that cuts of meat differ in Britain and France. (For example: There is no 'rump' cut of pork in Britain – see *'La Pointe'* on *Le Cochon* or *Le Porc*). Where a recipe specifies a cut that does not exist in British butchery, the best alternative has been suggested, in order not to complicate buying.

Le Boeuf
(Beef)

Until very recently the Périgord could have been likened to the English countryside of the last century, where the principal proteins for a man who preferred not to risk being hung for stealing a sheep or a lamb were bacon and eggs. The Périgordin returning home from the fields or from market might have expected to find a pot-au-feu (stuffed chicken boiled over the fire), but never a joint of roast beef – as explained in the section on Soups, a joint of beef might be bought as a mark of respect to the guests at a wedding or a communion, but such occasions come rarely in the life of a family. Even the Seigneurs regarded cattle as beasts of labour rather than as 'red meat' for the table.

Times have changed, but though one might suppose that the developments that have affected the agricultural landscape of Périgord might have influenced its cuisine, the culinary landscape remains unaltered. Despite the transition from the use of cattle in tillage to the tractor, beef continues to make a rare appearance on the tables of Périgord. This rarity has nothing to do with its availability. The remotest hamlets are visited weekly by mobile butchery shops selling the same wide variety of red meat cuts as may be bought in any large town. No, it has everything to do with that curious core of Périgordin individuality maintaining its customary balance between progress and tradition. It may also, perhaps, be due to an instinctive appreciation of what cannot be bettered – in Old England the opportunities for roasting an ox whole put the invention of ways of doing so into the realms of fantasy, and though in the farms of the Périgord Noir whence these recipes originate, little thought or ingenuity went into creating recipes for a meat one might eat only once or twice in a lifetime, the few recipes they did invent have become classic to the region.

Le Filet de Boeuf Sarladais
(Fillet of beef as in Sarlat)

Cooking time: 15 minutes to the lb and 15 minutes over

3–4 lb (1.5–2 kg) piece of beef fillet
2 truffles (more if you can spare them)
Enough thin rashers of streaky bacon to wrap the beef
1 glass of good white wine

2 or 3 tbsp eau-de-vie or similar alcohol
1 or 2 tbsp plain flour
½ oz (15 g) shallots, sliced
A knob of goose fat
Lardings
A little stock
Salt and pepper

To serve:
2 slices of toasted baguette per person
Pâté de foie gras

Preheat the oven to 400°F/200°C, Gas 6.
Spike the fillet of beef with the lardings. Wrap it in the thin rashers of streaky bacon. Scrub and peel the truffles. Cut one of them into 'cloves' (saving the parings) and spike the bacon with them. Season.
Stand the beef on a rack above a meat tin into which you have poured the white wine and eau-de-vie. Cook by weight (as indicated) in the preheated oven, basting with the liquid from the meat tin.
During this time, melt some goose fat in a pan and gently cook the sliced shallots. Sprinkle 1 or 2 tbsp of flour over the shallots and moisten with the liquid from the meat tin. Slice the second truffle and add it and the parings from the first truffle to this sauce. Add a little stock if necessary. Simmer for 5–10 minutes.

To serve: Slice and toast a baguette and spread a little pâté de foie gras on each slice. Place the joint on a hot dish and arrange the toast around it in a crown. Serve the sauce separately.

Le Boeuf Braisé aux Oignons
(Braised beef with onions)

Time: 5¼ hours
Serves 6–8

The word 'braise' means glowing coal or wood. Braising beef meant, originally, that the cooking pot stood in hot coals or wood embers with more hot coals piled on the lid. These would be renewed from the fire during the process of cooking to maintain the heat.

3 lb (1½ kg) joint of rump beef
4 oz (125 g) streaky bacon rashers
8 oz (250 g) lean veal
1½ glasses of white wine (1 per kg beef)
1 liqueur glass eau-de-vie or similar alcohol

20 small whole onions, as near as possible the same size
½ pint (300 ml) of stock
3 cloves of garlic
1 sugar lump, salt, pepper
Bouquet garni (1 sprig each thyme, parsley and bay)
Goose fat

Get the oven ready at 350°F, 180°C, Gas 4.

Slice one of the garlic cloves and spike the beef with the slices. Roll and string the beef. Cover the bottom of the casserole with rashers of streaky bacon, put the joint on top and add the slice of veal. Pour the wine and eau-de-vie over, set it alight and as the flames die down pour in the stock. Add the bouquet garni and 2 whole cloves of garlic. Season, including the lump of sugar. Cook in a moderate oven for 3½ hours.

Halfway through the cooking time brown the 20 small whole onions in some goose fat and add to the meat casserole. Continue cooking for another 1¾ hours. Baste frequently

To serve: Place the beef, bacon and veal on a heated dish surrounded by a crown of onions. Take the fat off the sauce and pour over the meats.

Note: This dish is usually eaten with either a 'pissenlit' salad or with La Mique (see p.26)

L'Entrecote Grillé à la Périgourdine
(Grilled steak à la Périgourdine)

The recipes in this book date from the days when the open fire was the only means of cooking. Grilling was done with a special type of handled gridiron with channels carrying the juices to a sort of long cup or pocket at the side. The modern charcoal barbecue makes a good substitute for the Périgord open fire, otherwise the grill of your cooker must suffice. The fire must be very hot, with no smoke.

Time: For a steak 1–1½ lb (500–700 g) and about 1 inch (2.5 cm) thick, allow 12 minutes

1–1½ lb (450–700 g) steak	Walnut oil
2 shallots, chopped finely with sprigs of parsley	Salt and pepper

Have the fire hot and ready. Put the grill to heat. Rub both sides of the steak with walnut oil. Put the meat on the grill and cook until a crust has formed that will hold in the juices. Don't allow the meat to come in direct contact with the fire. When the crust has formed, turn the steak and cook the other side. Test with a fine skewer; if it slides through easily, the meat is done. Remove from the fire, season with salt and pepper, and serve with the finely chopped shallots and parsley in the centre.

Serve with pommes de terre, frites à la persillade or with cèpes or French beans 'au hachis' (see Vegetables section).

Note: Fillet steak can also be cooked by this method but you will need more oil on the meat as it has less fat than entrecôte.

Le Queue de Boeuf au Vin Blanc
(Oxtail in white wine)

Oxtail was always cooked the day before it was eaten in Yorkshire, so that the fat could solidify and be removed before reheating. In Périgord, curiously considering the difference in temperature between the two zones, the fat is a relished part of the dish.

Time: 4 hours
Serves 4

1 oxtail	1 or 2 sticks of celery
Pork or goose fat	A few slices of pork rind or
Salt, pepper and allspice	rind/fat from bacon rashers
2 good-sized carrots	A large glass of white wine
2 good-sized onions	A little stock
1 turnip	

Preheat the oven to 300°F, 150°C, Gas 2.

Cut the oxtail in chunks and put it to soak in cold water for 2 hours or so.

Heat some pork fat in a pan, drain the pieces of oxtail and fry them in the pork fat, turning to brown each side. Arrange them in an ovenproof casserole and add seasoning and allspice. Chop up the carrots, onions, a turnip and a stick or two of celery, and add to the casserole. In Périgord one also puts in several slices of crackling, but, if that is impossible, substitute bacon rinds, cutting them from the rasher with about ½ an inch (1.2 cm) of fat on them. Pour over a large glass of white wine and a little stock – cover and cook in a very slow oven for 4 hours. Make sure the contents remain succulent; the oxtail should be moist but not swimming.

Le Veau
(Veal)

Les Côtes de Veau Farcies
(Stuffed veal chops)

Time: 20 minutes
Serves 6

An easy, quick, yet delicious dish.

6 veal chops of 8 oz (250 g) each	1 clove of garlic
6 oz (170 g) of streaky bacon, chopped	Parsley, chopped
	Salt and pepper
2 shallots, chopped	Lemon juice

Have the oven ready at 450°F, 230°C, Gas 8.

Make the stuffing by mincing together the bacon, garlic, shallots, parsley and seasoning.

Grill the chops under a hot grill for 5 minutes each side. Put them into an ovenproof dish, spread the stuffing over them and cook for 15 minutes or so in a hot oven.

Sprinkle with lemon juice just before serving.

L'Escalope de Veau au Truffe
(Veal scallops with truffle)

Time: 20 minutes
Serves 4

4 veal scallops
2 small or 1 large truffle (or a
    small tin of truffles)
2 oz (50 g) goose or pork fat

1 soupsp fresh cream
1 glass dry white wine
4 oz (125 g) plain flour
Salt and pepper

Salt, pepper and flour the scallops. Melt the goose or pork fat in a pan and cook the meat for 10 minutes. Turn and cook for a few more minutes. Add the fresh cream.

Cut the truffles in slices and heat them in the wine. (If you are using fresh truffles they will need to be cooked longer in the wine – about 20 minutes.) Add to the meat pan.

Serve the sauce poured over the meat.

La Rouelle de Veau Confite
(Casseroled Veal fillet)

Time: 2½ hours
Serves 6

4 lb (2 kg) of veal fillet
Goose or pork fat
4 oz (125 g) streaky bacon rashers
2 onions, each spiked with 2
    cloves
1 liqueur glass eau-de-vie or
    similar alcohol
2 carrots

3 or 4 shallots
Bouquet garni (1 sprig each of
    thyme, bay and parsley)
2 peeled, deseeded tomatoes or
    1 tbsp tomato purée
Salt and pepper
A little stock
Sorrel purée (see p. 120)

Brown the meat on both sides in the goose or pork fat. Cover the bottom of a casserole with streaky bacon and lay the meat on top. Put in the carrots, onions, shallots, herbs, salt, pepper and the glass of eau-de-vie, the tomatoes (if you are using purée, mix it with a little of the stock) and some stock. Cook for 2½ hours over a low flame or in a moderate oven (350°F, 180°C, Gas 4).

The liquid should be almost entirely absorbed, leaving only a thick juice with which to 'nappe' the meat.

To serve: Slice the veal, pour over the juices and serve with sorrel purée.

Les Alouettes sans Têtes
(Stuffed veal scallops)

Time: 30 minutes

This recipe, whose name means, literally, Skylarks without Heads, is typical of the Périgordines' skill in inventing a dish that brings together simple and sophisticated ingredients to perfection. The headless larks are veal scallops stuffed with pâté de foie gras and good things – a refined version of beef olives one might say. How much meat you buy depends on the thickness of the scallop and your estimation of your guests' appetites. Get the butcher to cut the scallops as thinly as possible and to flatten them for you as long and as wide as the average man's hand. (Do not be timid. Who knows? Your butcher may be an Artist Manqué, longing to exercise the refinements (yes, there are refinements) of butchery.)

Stuffing for 4 scallops:

1 or 2 tbsp pâté de porc, pâté de foie gras or grillons (see p. 114)

1 clove of garlic chopped finely with parsley

2 oz (50 g) breadcrumbs soaked in stock

1 egg yolk

Salt and pepper

2 or 3 veal scallops per person

4 streaky bacon rashers

A little goose or pork fat

To serve:

The same number of slices of toast as scallops

1 clove of garlic, crushed

Dampen the breadcrumbs with a little stock and squeeze out the excess liquid. Mix together the pâté of your choice or the grillons, the breadcrumbs, the chopped garlic and parsley and the seasoning. Bind with the egg yolk. Form the stuffing into sausages and place one in the centre of each scallop. Wrap the scallop round the sausage. Wrap a rasher of bacon round the scallop, arranging the two ends to resemble folded wings and tie up with string.

Melt some goose or pork fat and brown the 'birds without heads' all over. Cook for 20 minutes either in the oven (425°F, 220°C, Gas 7), under the grill – or on a charcoal fire. Turn during cooking.

To serve: Rub the slices of bread with the crushed garlic and toast. Serve the scallops on the toast with a little of the cooking juices poured over.

Le Roti de Veau aux Cèpes
(Roast veal with cèpes)

Another link with the kitchens of my childhood. Beef was roasted on a rack standing in the meat tin – the Yorkshire pudding was cooked *under* the meat and was served as an entrée. Cèpes cooked under the joint have all the same delicious impregnation of the juices as had those Yorkshire puddings.

Time: 15 minutes to the lb

A joint of roasting veal
1–2 lb (½–1 kg) sliced cèpes or whole mushrooms
Larding strips or streaky bacon rashers

A sauce Périgueux (see p. 117)
A slice of toast per person, rubbed with garlic
2 cloves of garlic, sliced

Heat oven to 400°F, 200°C, Gas 6.

Spike the joint of veal with sliced cloves of garlic. Put a layer of sliced cèpes (or whole mushrooms) into the roasting tin under the meat and roast in the usual manner, basting frequently. Make a sauce Périgueux. When the veal is ready, carve it in thickish slices, and serve on a hot dish on slices of toasted garlic bread with the cèpes around and the sauce Périgueux poured over.

Le Riz de Veau à la Sauce Périgueux
(Sweetbreads in sauce Périgueux)

I first learnt that balls were not only bounceable on overhearing my father inform a visitor that sweetbreads were calves' balls. He was wrong, of course: they are glands from the neck [the thymus gland] of the animal.

Sweetbreads à la sauce Périgueux, has the advantage that they can be cooked some time before you need them and be reheated; very useful if you are thinking of using them as an entrée.

Allow 6–8 oz (170–250 g) of sweetbreads per person
Goose or pork fat
1 truffle, sliced

1–2 slices of toast per person
A sauce Périgueux (see p. 117)
A knob of butter

Soak the sweetbreads in cold water for ½ an hour, then plunge into boiling water for a few minutes. Drain, wipe them and cut away the skin, etc., and fry gently in butter for 10–12 minutes. (At this stage precooked sweetbreads may be reheated.) Rub slices of bread with garlic, toast or fry the bread, and serve the sweetbreads on top garnished with slices of truffle and a sauce Périgueux.

Le Tripe de Veau à la Périgourdine
(Calves' tripe à la Périgourdine)

Time: 5 hours
Serves 6

3 lb (1.5 kg) of tripe
6 large or 12 small onions, sliced
6 large or 12 small carrots, sliced
A sprig each of thyme and bay
Salt and pepper
A calf's foot

2 or 3 rashers of streaky bacon or crackling
½ bottle dry white wine
A little water if needed
2 cloves garlic
Fresh parsley

I have not tasted this method of cooking calves' tripe, but it is said to be a fine dish – 'extra', as they say in Périgord.

There are still butchers in Britain with the 'calveage trade' touch who will clean and prepare the tripe ready for cooking. Ask for a calf's foot to be included and get the butcher to split it for you – calf's foot jelly has been highly regarded for centuries. Have the tripe cut in pieces of about 3 × 6 inches (7.5 × 15 cm). Roll these slices up and tie them firmly to avoid loss of shape during the lengthy cooking.

Slice several large onions and three carrots. Put them into the pot with thyme, a bay leaf, salt and pepper and add the rolled tied pieces of tripe, the split calf's foot and several pieces of crackling (pig's skin with some fat on it). Pour in half and half quantities of dry white wine and water and cook for 5 hours over a gentle but steady heat.

When you judge the tripe is ready, remove the calf's foot, the bay leaf and the sprig of thyme, pound some cloves of garlic with plenty of fresh parsley and serve the tripe rolls on garlic-rubbed slices of toast with the sauce (by this time thick and rich) poured over.

Le Mouton
(Mutton and Lamb)

Once upon a time the people of Périgord had an insurmountable revulsion for mutton and lamb. Barely a hundred years ago, it seems, they looked on lamb as an inferior meat. It is difficult to understand the reason for this repugnance, which can hardly have been based on the quality of the meat, since the breed of sheep raised in Périgord provides excellent joints. Whatever the reasons have been, the tables have turned, apparently, for there are few people in the region these days who do not enjoy a 'gigot' (leg of lamb) or a stuffed shoulder served in a sauce of rich nuances.

Le Gigot Périgourdin à la Couronne d'Ail
(Roast leg of lamb with a garlic crown)

Time: 15 minutes per pound and 15 minutes over

This is the dish Mme Tonneau cooked the day M. Tonneau's bank manager brought him the pike (see p. 67). Apart from beef, the Tonneaus' meat is all home-produced, killed and 'arranged'. M. Tonneau himself makes the pâtés and cures the hams.

These hams hang from the kitchen beams, and the day my first book was published I was treated to a slice. Mme Tonneau had to climb on the kitchen table to get it down, and I was myself affected by an almost insurmountable revulsion as M. Tonneau held the ham against his sheep-crotted jersey to carve the slice with a knife he found on the hen-crotted floor, a slice eventually wrapped in a piece of paper scrabbled out of the dresser drawer from among the nuts, bolts, old corks and string – what household hasn't such a drawer? I am glad I overcame my repugnance, because it was the most delicious ham I have ever tasted (and I did not go down with Salmonella).

As there were nine adults and several children to lunch that day, Mme Tonneau cooked *two* legs of lamb – which means, as you will see from the ingredients, that there were 100 cloves of garlic in the pan. *Do not* be alarmed by the quantity of garlic. By the end of the long, slow cooking they will have been transformed into succulent 'almonds' – and if you don't tell your guests what they are, I defy them to identify them as garlic.

4–5 lb (2–2½ kg) leg of lamb	50–60 whole cloves of garlic
2 tbsp goose or pork fat	2 good glasses of Sauterne or
1 liqueur glass of eau-de-vie or	Montbazillac
Cognac	Salt and pepper

Heat the fat and brown the meat all over. Put it into a meat tin with a lid. Separate and peel the garlic cloves and distribute them round the meat.

Pour over the glass of eau-de-vie, set alight and douse the flames with the 2 glasses of white wine, season and cover. Cook slowly and regularly (350°F 180°C, Gas 4) for the time as dictated by weight of joint. Baste frequently.

Serve the meat with the juices poured over, surrounded by its glorious crown of garlic.

It merits a St Emilion – and French beans or a crisp 'pissenlit' salad (see p.144) go well with the dish.

L'Épaule d'Agneau Sauté
(Sautéed shoulder of lamb)

Time: 40–50 minutes
Serves 4–6

1½ lb (700 g) shoulder of lamb, deboned and cut in medium-sized dice
4 oz (125 g) goose or pork fat
1½ lb (700 g) of cèpes, sliced

1 lb (500 g) small whole new potatoes
4 garlic cloves
A bunch of parsley
3 soupsp walnut or olive oil
Salt and pepper

Cut the earth end off the cèpe stalks, wash them briskly under water (do not allow them to stand in water, the flavour will be spoiled). Dry thoroughly and slice them. Scrape the potatoes. Peel the garlic and pound it with the parsley.

Heat 1 tbsp of goose fat and 1 soupsp of walnut/olive oil in a pan and brown the meat all over. When browned, reduce the heat, season and allow to continue cooking gently.

In another pan, heat 1 tbsp of goose fat and 1 soupsp of walnut/olive oil and brown the potatoes to a golden colour over a hot flame. When they are golden, cover, reduce the heat and leave to cook.

In another pan heat the rest of the goose fat and oil and cook the cèpes. Season.

When the potatoes and cèpes are cooked, add them to the meat pan. Throw in the garlic and parsley 'hachis', raise the heat under the pan, and allow to cook for a few more minutes.

To serve: Heat a dish. Arrange the lamb and cépes in the centre and the potatoes round the edge.

A good Fronsac goes well with this dish.

Le Cou de Môuton Grillé
(Grilled neck of mutton)

Time: 2½ hours to cook the mutton, 20 minutes for the transformation.
Serves 4

The name of this dish will surprise those who know how long it takes to cook neck of mutton. (One day, perhaps, I will write a book giving *A Taste of Yorkshire*. There were four ovens in our coal-fire kitchen range, the top left-hand oven being for slow cooking. Neck of mutton was cooked in this oven, sometimes overnight, in a closed dish and on a bed of carrots, onions, celery and herbs but very little water. It was allowed to go cold, the fat was taken off, the dish was reheated – it was delicious! It was brown, and crisp and scrumptious – very unlike the general idea of neck of mutton.)

This particular recipe is useful for two reasons: neck of mutton is not an expensive cut of meat and it can be cooked the day before you want to *transform* it into a rather unusual dish for guests.

For 4 people you will need an entire neck of mutton. Ask the butcher to cut each half neck into 4.

1 neck of mutton, cut into 8 pieces	3 garlic cloves
2 glasses of dry white wine	Bouquet garni (thyme, tarragon, parsley and bay leaf)
3 carrots, cut in chunks	4 oz (125 g) breadcrumbs, toasted
1 large onion, stuck with a clove	2 soupsp of walnut or olive oil
1 large stick of celery, chopped	Salt and pepper

For the sauce:
1 tbsp of old-fashioned mustard   Salt and pepper
1 glass of walnut oil

Put all the ingredients except those for the sauce, the breadcrumbs and oil into a casserole. Just cover with water and add the wine. Cover and cook for 2½ hours (325°F, 170°C, Gas 3).

When the meat is cooked, remove it from the broth and if you are going to use it at once, dry it carefully and set it aside. The broth is not needed for this recipe. (In Périgord they have an insurmountable aversion to lamb-based soups.)

Get the grill very hot. Cover the meat with oil, roll it in the toasted breadcrumbs and cook under the hot grill for 20 minutes. Turn to brown on all sides.

The sauce:
Thin the mustard with the oil, drop by drop, as when making a mayonnaise. Season. Serve separately.

Les Côtelettes d'Agneau à la Purée d'Asperges
(Lamb cutlets with asparagus purée)

Time: 20 minutes. The sauce can be made while the cutlets are cooking.

As many cutlets as you require (2 lamb or 1 veal per person)

Purée for 4–6 servings:
2 lb (1 kg) asparagus	Salt and pepper
2 tbsp plain flour	Parsley, chervil and chives, finely
½ pint (300 ml) milk	chopped

Tie the asparagus in bundles and cook in boiling salted water. Drain and cut away the woody part of the stalk. Gradually blend the flour and milk together, heat and stir while it thickens. Remove from the flame and add the asparagus. Either put through a coarse sieve or blend in an electric blender or food processor. When the cutlets are grilled, serve with the purée over them, sprinkled with the chopped herbs.

L'Agneau Rôti
(Roast lamb)

(Another recipe for the enthusiast.)
First kill your lamb … I will go no further with my instructions on skinning, cleaning, etc. In fact, the lamb is cooked whole, wrapped in waxed paper, either over the fire or in the oven. Towards the end of the cooking time, a sauce of finely chopped shallots blended with the juices from the meat is prepared, and the whole lamb is arranged on a long dish garnished with parsley, with the sauce served separately.

This is not the recipe for anyone who prefers to forget that the meat they are enjoying was gambolling among the buttercups not so long ago. It is very Périgourdin, however.

Les Côtelettes aux Châtaignes
(Chops with chestnuts)

Time: Chestnuts 45 minutes. Chops 40 minutes

As many cutlets as you require (2 lamb or 1 veal per person)
8 oz (225 g) of chestnuts per person
Stock to cook the chestnuts
A knob of butter

Salt and pepper
1 garlic clove, crushed, per person
A little sugar if necessary
A little parsley to garnish

Shell the chestnuts and cook them in stock for about 45 minutes. When cooked, beat into a purée with some butter, salt and pepper. A little sugar can be added, if you think that this blends well with the lamb.

Rub the chops with salt and crushed garlic. Grill them, turning them halfway through the cooking time.

Serve with the chestnut sauce, garnished with parsley.

Le Cochon
(Pork)

I have previously mentioned the similarities between Yorkshire and the Périgord. The title of this section and its English substitute represent one of the differences between the two regions. For centuries, *Le Cochon* has been synonymous with meat in Périgord, and to this day it is rarely called Porc (Pork). In the north of England, the word P.I.G. either has to be spelled out or wood must be touched as you say it. Why? One is reminded of the Graham Greene character who was killed in South America by a pig falling from a balcony, and though, according to *Farmers' Weekly*, more people are killed by attacks from pigs than by tractor or other accidents in farming, the P.I.G. surely brings us greater benefits than disasters. One day I must research the origins of this northern superstition.

Almost every household in rural Périgord fattens a pig, and those who haven't the chance to rear the animal themselves pay a farmer to do so. The pig is killed between December and spring along with the fattened poultry, doubtless because work in the fields is at its minimum during that period and work on the pig requires a maximum of effort – I haven't come upon a recipe for the eyeballs, but every other part of the animal has its proper arrangement. The continuing importance of *Le Cochon* in the life of Périgord, despite hypermarkets and private vehicles, is further proof of the deep-rooted sense of tradition and a profound identification with *Le Pais* – 'I can't come this week,' the plumber told me when a radiator sprang a leak at −20°C, 'we're killing the pig'. The post office closes while the post mistress kills her pig, the baker keeps eccentric hours when his pig is being killed, the dustman barely mentions the weather when it's his pig's turn. *Le Cochon* is a way of life. The charcuterie of Périgord is world famous and it is dealt with in *Les Confits* (Conserves, see p. 111). This section concerns fresh pork meat.

L'Enchaud Périgourdin
(Rolled fillet of pork)

Time: 12 hours 'rest' before 2½ hours of cooking
Serves 6–8

The 'Enchaud' (an untranslatable Périgourdin word) is a very old dish. In this particular corner of Périgord Noir, the joint (our loin of pork) is not boned – so, of course, it can't be rolled. Here it is incorrect to use the term 'Enchaud' for boned meat – which only goes to emphasize the individuality of the Périgordins: Not only do they distinguish themselves from the rest of France, they distinguish themselves from Périgordins fifty miles away. It is evidently correct to call this recipe 'L'Enchaud Périgourdin' because it was created within the boundaries of Périgord, but it is not what the Périgordins of *my* area call an 'Enchaud'.

Well, this is an old Périgourdin recipe that has played a useful part for centuries, particularly because it is almost better served cold, which can't be said of many regional dishes. During the grape harvest (the 'vendange') for instance, itinerant workers are taken on to pick the grapes (much as the East-Enders traditionally invade the hop fields of Kent at hop-picking time) and slices of cold 'enchaud' on bread with a gherkin on top is one of the delights of the vendangeurs. The fat and jelly from the meat is frequently served on toast with aperitifs (Bread-and-Dripping à la Périgourdine).

There are two parts to this recipe, the first being the simple L'Enchaud Périgourdin' and the second the L'Enchaud Truffé'.

L'Enchaud Périgourdin

3 lb (1.5 kg) boned fillet of pork (if the butcher is boning loins of pork, ask for the bones as well)
A sprig of thyme

4 garlic cloves, peeled and sliced
2 soupsp pork fat
¼–½ pint (150–300 ml) stock
Salt and pepper

Preheat the oven to 350°F, 180°C, Gas 4.

Spread out the meat and spike it with the sliced garlic cloves. Season with salt and freshly ground pepper. Roll up the meat tightly and tie it very firmly. Put it in a cool place to 'repose' until next day. (This 'repose' is an important part in the 'Enchaud' but no one can give a reason for it.)

When you are ready to begin cooking, heat the pork fat and brown the meat all over for 25–30 minutes. When the meat is nicely browned pour over the stock, add the thyme, salt and pepper, put aluminium foil over the casserole and cover with a lid. Cook in the oven for 2 hours.

L'Enchaud aux Truffes

For the stuffed version, a dish used in the time of the Revolution, you will need in addition to the above:

1 lb (500 g) of sausage-meat	¼–½ pint (150–300 ml) stock
2 truffles, cleaned and sliced	Salt and pepper

Time: Allow 20 minutes per lb and 20 minutes over.

Preheat the oven to 350°F, 180°C, Gas 4.

Scrub, peel and slice the truffles. Open the meat out and spread with the sausage meat. Spike the sausage-meat evenly with slices of truffle. Roll the meat up and tie firmly. Melt the fat in an ovenproof casserole, put in the enchaud and pour over the stock. Put in the oven. When it is cooked, remove the string, defat the juices by skimming off the fat and serve them separately.

If you wish to use the enchaud cold, lift it out of the juices when it is cooked, cut off the string, and put the joint in a cool place. In the old days the enchaud was kept for some time coated in pork fat: it is thought to be better when not cut into immediately.

Le Porc aux Châtaignes
(Pork with chestnuts)

Time: 2–2½ hours
Serves 6

3 lb (1.5 kg) roasting joint of pork	½ pint (300 ml) lukewarm water
Pork fat to brown the outside of the meat	2 garlic cloves
	1 lb (500 g) chestnuts
6 small onions, peeled	Salt and pepper

Preheat the oven to 375°F, 190°C, Gas 5.

In an ovenproof casserole, heat the pork fat and brown the meat all over. When it is a good brown, add the water, salt and pepper, the whole onions and the garlic. Cover and cook in a moderate oven for 2 hours.

While the meat is cooking, roast the chestnuts under the grill for about 5 minutes. Peel them and, when the meat has been cooking for an hour or so, add them to the casserole.

To serve: Take the fat off the juices, arrange the meat on a hot platter with the onions and chestnuts round it. Pour the defatted gravy over.

Le Foie de Porc Farci
(Stuffed liver of pork)

Time: 40–50 minutes
Serves 4–6

This dish is best made with a whole liver but if you can only find liver already sliced allow 2–3 slices per person.

1 whole pig's liver (approx. 2 lb (1 kg))	3 cloves garlic
	Parsley
1 lb (500 g) sliced onions	Lemon juice
1 lb (500 g) tomatoes, quartered and skinned	Pork fat

For the stuffing:

1 lb (500 g) sausage-meat	chopped
2–3 oz (50–80 g) breadcrumbs	1 egg, beaten
1 onion and 3 or 4 shallots, finely	Salt and pepper

Heat the oven to 350–375°F, 180–190°C, Gas 4–5.

Make the stuffing from the sausage-meat, onion, shallots, 2 cloves of garlic sliced, seasoning, breadcrumbs and the beaten egg.

If you have succeeded in getting a whole liver, make incisions over the surface and push the stuffing into the slits. If you have sliced liver, form the stuffing into sausages and wrap the liver round them. In either case, tie up the stuffed liver during cooking.

Peel and slice 1 lb (450 g) onions. Melt the pork fat and put in the onions. Skin the tomatoes, cut into quarters, and add to the pan with the onions. When they are softened, transfer to an ovenproof, lidded casserole, put in the stuffed liver, cover firmly and cook in a moderate oven for 40–50 minutes (a little less if you have used sliced liver). Crush the third garlic clove with some parsley and add to the casserole 10 minutes before the end of the cooking time.

To serve: Remove the string. Arrange on a heated dish and trickle lemon or verjuice over. Exquisite!

Les Pieds de Porc en Civet
(Jugged trotters)

Time: 3–3½ hours
Serves 8

8 trotters	8 walnuts, shelled
8 oz (250 g) streaky bacon	3 bottles of Cahors
6 carrots, chopped	Salt and pepper
3 onions, chopped	Goose or pork fat
4 garlic cloves, chopped	Flour for thickening the sauce
3 cloves, thyme and a bay leaf	A small onion
A few juniper berries	

To serve: slices of bread rubbed with crushed garlic

Heat the goose fat. Cut the trotters in 3 and brown in the fat. Add the carrots, onions and garlic. When they have all taken on a good colour, sprinkle with flour and gradually pour in the wine, which must completely cover the trotters. Add the thyme, bay leaf and cloves (stuck in a small onion), the juniper berries and the shelled walnuts. Season. Cook for 3½ hours over a low flame.

To serve: Test the seasoning. Rub slices of bread with crushed garlic and arrange round the dish of trotters.

Les Côtelettes de Porc aux Salsifis
(Pork cutlets with salsify sauce)

Time: 1 hour

Salsify is a popular vegetable in Périgord, particularly the wild or black salsify (see p. 137), a popularity probably engendered by the belief that it is good for the liver.

4 pork cutlets

For the sauce:

1–1½ lb (500–700 g) salsify
1 onion, chopped
2 seeded, tomatoes or 1 tbsp
    tomato purée
A knob of goose or pork fat

Salt, pepper and a pinch of
    allspice
1–2 tbsp plain flour
A little stock

Scrape and clean the salsify and put into boiling, salted water to cook for 20 minutes.

While it is cooking, heat the goose fat and gently brown the sliced onion and tomatoes/purée. Sprinkle with flour and gradually stir in the stock to a creamy consistency.

Drain the salsify and add to the other ingredients. Allow to simmer a little longer, stirring.

Cook the cutlets under the grill or over a charcoal fire for at least 10 minutes per side. While they are cooking sieve/blend the sauce and put in a pan to reheat.

Serve the cutlets garnished with the sauce.

Le Gibier
(Game)

The Périgord, perhaps more than any other region of France, has always been rich in game and *La Chasse* (hunting) is enthusiastically, *passionately* even, pursued to this day, each commune having its proper border with territorial rights. The deer don't know this, of course, but its end will be the same whether it moves from east to west or west to east, for the moment a front hoof crosses a border into another territory the deer becomes the 'property' of that commune.

Every commune is supposed to restrict the carnage to a certain number of deer each year, generally the first four Sundays of the season which starts in September being the chances of reaching the target. If no deer have been shot by the end of the fourth Sunday – then that year's chances have gone and all that remains to the hunters are the rabbits and hares or an occasional woodcock. On paper, the season is strictly controlled, even the hour when the day's shooting may begin being written into the permit (which currently costs £100 per hunter for a short season's shooting). I can set my watch on chasse days by the first shot fired from the plateau above me where M. Tonneau's son, Denis, has been waiting, eye to his shotgun sight, for the hour to strike.

Towards the beginning of November a marquee (*un dancing*) is set up in the village square and 200 or more people sit down to the lengthy Repas des Chasseurs (the Hunters' Banquet) to enjoy the spoils of the hunt. The old recipes from long ago have been carefully guarded, and the chef or 'traiteur' of the banquet has the unenviable job of executing the recipes for the approval of two hundred knowledgeable diners.

There are no recipes for venison – four-legged game for the domestic table is limited to hares and rabbits, the deer being a 'protected' species to be consumed publicly. No doubt there is a saying in patois on the risks of being hung for a stag or a deer. In my researches I came upon one recipe for roasting a small deer, simply saying: 'Bleed and skin the beast, cut off its head and feet and put it in the oven with all the herbs on which it has been reared.'

This section has been divided into two: recipes for furred game followed by recipes for feathered game.

Note: Game pâtés and terrines will be found on pp. 57–64.

FURRED GAME

Marinade for Game

1 bottle of red wine	2 cloves
1 glass of wine vinegar	4 garlic cloves
2 tbsp walnut or olive oil	10 juniper berries
8 oz (250 g) carrots, chopped	Thyme, bay leaf, sage and
4 oz (125 g) onions, sliced	rosemary
2 oz (50 g) shallots	Salt and pepper
6 peppercorns	

Put all the above into a deep earthenware dish. Put in the rabbit or hare, either whole or chopped, depending on the recipe. Turn the meat several times during the day. Leave in a cool place for 48 hours before you intend to start cooking.

Le Lapin Farci (Stuffed rabbit)

Time: 1½ hours
Serves 4–6

3–4 lb (1½–2 kg) rabbit	2 cloves garlic
8 oz (250 g) sausage-meat	½ pint (300 ml) dry white wine
4 oz (125 g) breadcrumbs	1 onion, chopped
2 eggs	1 carrot, chopped
1½ glasses water	2 oz (50 g) goose fat
1 tbsp chopped parsley	Bouquet garni

Heat the oven to 375°F, 190°C, Gas 5.

Begin by preparing the stuffing. Chop up the rabbit's liver. Mix it with the sausage-meat, chopped parsley, breadcrumbs, seasoning and bind with the eggs.

Remove the rabbit's head and feet. Fill the stomach with the stuffing and sew it up.

Heat the fat in an ovenproof casserole and brown the rabbit on all sides. Add the chopped onion and carrot, pour over the wine and water and put in the garlic and the bouquet garni. Cover. Cook for 1½ hours.

To serve: Remove rabbit from the casserole and keep it hot. Reduce the juices of the sauce, remove the bouquet garni, put into the blender. Serve this sauce separately.

Le Lapin aux Câpres
(Rabbit with capers)

Time: 1½ hours
Serves 4–6

2–3 lb (1–1½ kg) rabbit	The juice of a lemon
1 oz (30 g) butter	A handful of capers
1 oz (30 g) plain flour	Bouquet garni
1 glass of water	1 onion, sliced
1 egg yolk	Salt and pepper
4 fl. oz (100 ml) fresh cream	

Cut off the head and feet of the rabbit. Cut the rabbit into pieces. Heat the butter and brown the rabbit all over. Slice the onion and add to the pan. Toss in the bouquet garni and season. Sprinkle with the flour and moisten with the water. Cover and allow to simmer gently over a low flame for 1 hour. Turn the meat during this time.

After cooking for an hour, add the capers and continue cooking for 20 minutes. Beat the egg yolk into the cream and pour over the rabbit. *Do not* let it boil from now on.

To serve: Arrange the rabbit on a hot dish, pour over the lemon juice and serve at once.

Le Civet de Lièvre Périgourdin
(Hare in red wine)

Time: 3–4 hours, depending on age and size of hare
Serves 6

5 lb (2.5 kg) hare
Goose or pork fat for browning
    the hare
Marinade (see p. 96)

6 oz (170 g) streaky bacon
2 tbsp plain flour
1 bottle good red wine
Salt and pepper

Cut off the head and feet of the hare and discard. Cut the hare into joints. Put the pieces into the marinade and leave in a cool place for 48 hours.

Lift out the hare and dry it. Strain the marinade through a muslin cloth and keep both the liquid and the solids in the muslin.

Heat the goose or pork fat in a casserole and brown the hare joints all over. Chop the bacon rashers into small pieces and brown with the hare. Sprinkle flour over these meats, moistening with the liquid from the marinade.

Pour a bottle of good red wine into a saucepan, heat it and set it alight. When the flame dies, pour it over the hare. Tie up the muslin cloth you have strained the marinade in and add to the casserole. Cover and cook very slowly for 3–4 hours.

Remove muslin wrapping. Allow to go cold, take off the fat and reheat gently when you are ready to use.

Serve with rice.

Note: A civet is always better if used the day after you have cooked it.

Le Lapin en Papillotes
(Rabbit packets)

Time: 45–60 minutes
Serves 4

1 young rabbit

Stuffing:

4 oz (125 g) streaky bacon
2 garlic cloves
1 onion
2–3 sprigs of parsley

2 egg yolks
6 oz (170 g) sausage-meat
4 oz (125 g) mushrooms
Salt and pepper

Preheat the oven to 375°F, 190°C, Gas 5.

Mince all the stuffing ingredients together and bind with the egg yolks.

Cut off the rabbit's head and feet. Divide the body into 8 portions. Have ready 8 pieces of buttered foil. Spread the stuffing on the rabbit pieces and wrap them in the foil. Place the packets into an oven-proof dish and cook for 45–60 minutes depending on the age of the rabbit.

Le Lapereau Rôti à la Broche
(Young rabbit, spit-roasted)

Time: 60 minutes
Serves 4

A young rabbit
Salt and pepper
4 rashers streaky bacon
Parsley, thyme, rosemary and 3
    juniper berries, chopped

½ pint (300 ml) stock
2 oz (50 g) goose or pork fat
1 lb (500 g) cooked chestnuts
2 garlic cloves, crushed with
    parsley

Preheat the oven to 375°F, 190°C, Gas 5.

Cut off the head and feet of the rabbit. Season the interior with salt and pepper. Make a stuffing with 2 rashers of streaky bacon, 1 sprig each of parsley, thyme, rosemary and 3 juniper berries, chopped together. Stuff the rabbit and sew up the stomach. Tie 2 bacon rashers round the body, tieing the legs under the rashers. Fix the rabbit on to the spit, either in the oven or over an open fire, with a pan underneath. Pour the stock and goose fat into the pan and baste frequently for about an hour, depending on age and size of the rabbit. (Rabbit is a dry meat which needs frequent basting.) Halfway through the cooking time, put the chestnuts into the dripping pan under the rabbit.

To serve: Remove the stitches. Pound the garlic and parsley. Arrange the rabbit on a hot dish with the chestnuts around, garnish with the garlic and parsley. Potatoes cut in pieces also go very well, cooked under the rabbit.

LE GIBIER AUX PLUMES
(GAME BIRDS)

Le Perdreau Farci au Foie Gras
(Partridge with foie gras stuffing)

Time: 45 minutes
Serves 4

2 partridges
8 oz (250 g) foie gras or pâté de
    foie gras
½ pint (300 ml) eau-de-vie or
    similar alcohol

½ pint (300 ml) port
2 oz (50 g) truffle
Walnut or olive oil
4 rashers of streaky bacon
Salt and pepper

Note: If you are using pâté de foie gras you will need only 1 truffle.

Preheat the oven to 375°F, 190°C, Gas 5.

Season the inside of the birds. Stuff them with the foie gras mixed with sliced truffle or with the pâté de foie gras. Wrap the streaky bacon over the birds and roast in a moderate oven for 45 minutes.

When cooked, remove the partridges from the roasting dish, put them into a terrine and keep hot while you make the sauce as follows.

Degrease the roasting tin by tipping out the fat and wiping the sides of the tin. Pour in the port and the eau-de-vie and reduce over a fast flame. Pour the reduced liquid over the birds, raise the heat of the oven to 450°F, 230°C, Gas 8 and glaze the birds.

Serve very hot.

Salmis de Pintarde
(Ragoût of guinea-fowl)

There are several ways of cooking a ragôut of game. It may be made with red or white wine and in some regions cream is added at the end of the cooking. The bird is always roasted first, and then finished in the sauce.

This recipe is equally good with teal, snipe, pheasant, doves and woodcocks.

Time: 1½ hours
Serves 6–8

2 guinea-fowl (2 lb/1 kg each)	1 pint (575 ml) white wine
4 oz (125 g) butter	8 oz (250 g) mushrooms
4 oz (125 g) onions, sliced	Bouquet garni
3 oz (80 g) carrots, chopped	2 pt (1 l) chicken stock
1½ oz (40 g) plain flour	1 small glass Cognac
1 tbsp goose fat	Salt and pepper

Preheat the oven to 400°F, 200°C, Gas 6.

Melt the butter in an ovenproof dish, put in the birds and brown them all over. Put them into the preheated oven to cook for 15–20 minutes. Remove the birds and cut them into quarters.

Turn down the oven to 375°F, 190°C, Gas 5, leaving the dish in. Put the onions and carrots into the dish to sweat. Return the quartered birds to the oven, having dusted them with flour and cook for 5 minutes. Gradually pour in the wine and stock, add the bouquet garni and continue cooking for 30 minutes.

Clean and slice the mushrooms and fry them in the goose fat. Add them to the guinea-fowl.

Heat the Cognac, set it alight, then douse it with the juices from the oven. Put the liquid through a fine sieve or blender. Return to the ovenproof dish and continue cooking for a further 15–20 minutes.

Le Faisan aux Cèpes Farcis
(Pheasant with stuffed cèpes)

Time: 1¼ hours
Serves 4

1 pheasant
3 rashers of streaky bacon
1 lb (500 g) sausage-meat
2 lb (1 kg) cèpes
½ teacup stock
1 teacup breadcrumbs
2 soupsp milk
6 oz (170 g) poultry liver (includ-

ing the pheasant's liver)
6 shallots, finely sliced
4 garlic cloves, crushed
Parsley and thyme
Salt and pepper
1 egg, beaten
A knob of butter
Walnut or olive oil

[When the pheasant is cleaned, make sure you have the liver; make up the weight required with other game or poultry liver.]

Heat some butter in a pan and turn the livers in it for 3 minutes. Put them through a mincer.

Cut off the earth end of the cèpe stalks and separate from the heads. Slice the stalks finely. Add 2 soupspoons of walnut or olive oil to the butter in the pan. Brown the shallots and add the cèpe stalks, moving them about with a wooden spoon.

Heat the oven to 450°F, 230°C, Gas 8.

Mix together the sausage-meat, livers, shallots and cèpe stalks, pounded garlic, parsley and thyme, salt and pepper, milk and breadcrumbs and bind with the beaten egg. Put some of this stuffing into the cèpe heads and stuff the pheasant with the remains of the mixture.

Grease an ovenproof dish and butter the bird. Cook it in the oven for half an hour. Then arrange the stuffed cèpes round the pheasant, trickle a little oil over them and continue the cooking. Fry the bacon and add it and its fat to the pheasant.

To serve: Reduce the cooking juices and serve separately from the bird.

Les Pigeoneaux aux Petits Pois
(Young pigeons with fresh peas)

Time: 30 minutes for the birds and 30 minutes for the peas.
Serves 6.

Note: As will be seen from the recipe the two dishes are cooked separately.

6 young pigeons	2 sugar lumps
6 rashers of streaky bacon	3 oz (80 g) carrots, peeled and
4 oz (125 g) of goose fat	finely sliced
2 lb (1 kg) shelled peas	4 oz (125 g) piece of salt pork
2 oz (50 g) little onions, peeled	Salt and pepper

Season the insides of the pigeons. Wrap the bacon over them and brown in the goose fat. Cover and leave to cook for 30 minutes, basting frequently.

Cut the salt pork into dice and fry. Add the finely sliced carrots and the little onions, and leave to sweat for 5 minutes. Add the fresh, shelled peas, a little pepper, the sugar lumps and a glass of water. Cover and leave to cook for half an hour.

To serve: Arrange the pigeons on a hot dish with the peas and salt pork round them. Trickle over the juices from the two pans.

Les Cailles à la Périgourdine
(Quails à la Périgourdine)

Time: Allow 1 hour to prepare this dish the day before you wish to cook it. Cooking time 40 minutes.
Serves 4

6 quails	2 lb (1 kg) meat jelly
2 oz (50 g) of foie gras	2 egg yolks
6 oz (170 g) game or poultry	2 tbsp fresh cream
livers	4 fl. oz (125 ml) white port
6 oz (170 g) streaky bacon	2 fl. oz (50 ml) Cognac
A small truffle, finely chopped	A pinch of allspice
2 tbsp butter	Salt and pepper

You will need a piece of muslin to wrap the quails in.

Get the butcher to bone the birds (note: keep the livers). Cut the bacon into small pieces and fry for 3 minutes. Remove from the pan. Make sure the fat is very hot and put in the livers to firm them. Remove them from the pan.

Pour a little of the port into the pan and scrape the pan with a wooden spoon to get the meat juices into the port. Put in the chopped truffle and leave to simmer for 5 minutes. Allow to cool.

Flatten 4 of the boned quails, skin down, on to a clean cloth. Salt and pepper them. Sprinkle them with the Cognac, roll them up, and leave them like this throughout the rest of the preparations.

Cut the meat from the two remaining quails into small pieces. Put them, the bacon and the livers through a mincer. Add the foie gras. Mix the egg yolks into the port and truffles. Stir in the cream. Make a homogenous stuffing from this liquid and the minced quail, bacon and livers. Season with a pinch of allspice, salt and pepper.

Now return to the whole boned quails. Open them out flat. Divide the stuffing into 4 and put a quarter of it on to each quail. Fold up the birds again, and sew them to ensure that the stuffing does not escape. Cut 4 pieces of muslin, large enough to wrap the quails in. Tie them in firmly at both ends. Melt the jelly in a pan, adding half the remaining port. Bring to boiling point and plunge the four wrapped birds into the liquid. Leave to simmer for 25 minutes. At the end of this time withdraw the pan from the heat, pour in the rest of the port and leave the birds to cool in the liquid jelly.

When cold, but before the jelly has set, take out the birds. Remove the muslin, wipe the birds thoroughly, and stand them in a terrine. Strain the jelly and pour over the quails. They should be completely covered by the jelly. Leave it to set. If necessary put in a refrigerator but *not* in a deep freeze.

Serve cold.

Les Becassines aux Cèpes
(Snipe with cèpes)

If you are hesitating over a wine with this recipe try a red Graves.

Time: 1¼ hours
Serves 6

6 snipe
2 lb (1 kg) cèpes
1 cabbage with a lot of heart
8 oz (250 g) streaky bacon
Thyme
½ glass Armagnac
1 teacup breadcrumbs
2–3 tbsp stock
6 oz (170 g) butter

2 soupsp walnut or olive oil
4 garlic cloves
Parsley
3 bay leaves
4 shallots, chopped
6 lean slices of ham
1 egg
3 spring onions
Salt and pepper

Clean the cèpes without standing in water. Wash the cabbage and reserve 12 good leaves, chopping the remainder.

Cut the bacon into small pieces and put into a casserole of cold water. Bring to the boil, simmer for 5 minutes, drain, and allow to go cold. When cold, put the lardings through the mincer.

Heat 2 tbsp of butter and 1 tbsp of oil. Chop the cèpe stalks and put into the heated fat. Leave them until the water has evaporated, then brown them. Add half the minced lardings.

Chop together the garlic, parsley and shallots. Add half to the cèpe stalks. Season and stir over a high flame for 2 minutes, then remove from the heat. Moisten the breadcrumbs with the stock and squeeze out any excess liquid. Clean and chop the spring onions.

Make the stuffing by mixing the cèpes-and-larding mixture with the breadcrumbs and spring onions. Bind with the beaten egg and add a soupspoon of Armagnac, chopped thyme and seasoning.

Plunge the cabbage leaves into boiling salted water for 3 minutes. Drain and wipe dry. Arrange 2 leaves, one on top of the other. Divide the stuffing between the 6 pairs of leaves. Roll them into tight packets and put each into a slice of ham. Slide them into each of the snipe. Heat 2 oz (50 g) butter in a pan and brown the other half of minced lardings. Add the chopped cabbage, season and cover until soft. Leave to simmer – and make sure the cabbage does not stick to the bottom of the pan.

Divide the bay leaves in two and spike each bird with half a leaf. Heat the rest of the butter and brown the birds on all sides. Cover the pan and cook them for 20 minutes.

In another pan, heat the rest of the oil and 1 soupspoon of butter. Put in the cèpe heads, season and leave to cook gently, turning them over halfway through the cooking. When you judge they are cooked (usually 15–20 minutes, but test with a fork), sprinkle the other half of the garlic, parsley and shallots over them, and cook for one more minute. Keep hot.

When the birds are à point, pour over the remaining Armagnac and set it alight.

To serve: Arrange the 6 best cèpe-heads in the centre of a heated platter. Place a bird on each cèpe-head, with alternate spoonfuls of the cabbage-and-cèpe mixtures surrounding them.

Les Surprises de Périgueux
(Périgueux surprises)

Time: This is guess-work. Depending on the bird of your choice – probably 30–45 minutes.
Serves 6

This recipe was given to me more as a gastronomic curiosity than as a serious example of *La Cuisine Périgourdine*. It would not be found on the everyday tables of the region and I hand it on to you in the same spirit in which I received it. I haven't tasted it – nor have I met anyone who has – but it sounds absolutely delicious and it could be adapted to easier birds to handle than those listed, such as pheasant or partridge, without altering the gamy flavour of the dish.

6 quails, 6 grebe or 12 larks
Salt and pepper

A good glass of Cognac
1 lb (500 g) short-crust pastry

For the 'essence':
The bones of the birds, crushed
1 soup ladle of water or stock

1 soup ladle of Madeira
Thyme, salt and pepper

For the stuffing:
The livers of the birds, minced
4 rashers of streaky bacon,
    minced
2 heaped tbsp of breadcrumbs

12 peeled mushrooms, finely
    chopped
6 truffles, sliced
1 egg

Preheat the oven to 400°F, 200°C, Gas 6.

Bone the birds you have selected (keep the bones and livers). Put the meat into a terrine, sprinkle with salt and pepper and pour over the Cognac. Leave them to marinate, turning occasionally.

Make the short-crust pastry and set aside in a cool place.

Mince all the ingredients for the stuffing, except the truffles, and bind with the egg. When you are ready to make the 'surprises', add the Cognac from the marinade to the stuffing.

Roll out the pastry very thinly, and cut it into rounds large enough to take a sixth of the above ingredients. Form the pastry into cones, and fill each cone with slices of truffle, a spoonful of stuffing, the meat of 1 quail, 1 grebe, or 2 larks, a second spoonful of stuffing and some final slices of truffle. Dampen the edges of the pastry and seal up the cone.

Place the 'surprises' in an ovenproof dish and cook them for 30–45 minutes (only the cook can decide).

Meanwhile, make an 'essence' from the bones. Crush the bones and put them into a pan with a ladle of water, a ladle of Madeira, a sprig of thyme and a little seasoning. Leave to simmer while the birds are cooking.

To serve: Strain the 'essence' through a muslin cloth, squeezing out all the juices. Reheat the essence and as each guest opens his 'surprise' moisten the interior with this 'sauce'.

Les Volailles
(Poultry)

It is no wonder that poultry in Périgord is famed for its high quality and delicate flavour, for, apart from that brief period when they are being fattened for pâté and conserves, the birds run free to peck and choose from the natural resources of their field or other open-air enclosure. No bird could hope for more, but more is given to them – a supplementary bonus of the maize that grows so well in Périgord's soil – and that adds a bonus to the flavour of their flesh.

There is no distinctively Périgourdin way of roasting poultry, but the truffle, the cèpes and the chestnut bring a distinctly Périgourdin flavour to the stuffings (although Mme Robert uses no other garnish for her roasted poultry than a piece of bread spiked with garlic cloves, put inside the birds to waft the 'parfum' into their flesh). Since most of the stuffings given for game birds in the preceding section can be used for poultry, this section has been devoted to some other ways of cooking domestic birds in Périgord.

La Galantine de Dinde Truffée
(Galantine of turkey with truffles)

Time: 3 hours actual cooking, plus 48 hours for the weighting of the galantine
Serves 10–12

This is an excellent way of serving turkey and is useful for making an old bird acceptable.

1 boned turkey (around 10 lb
    [4.5 kg])

For the stock:

Enough water or stock to cover the boned bird	3 peppercorns
2 onions stuck with 3 cloves each	A bouquet garni of thyme, rosemary, bay and sage
2 good-sized carrots, sliced	A glass of port

For the stuffing:

The bird's liver, minced	3 truffles, sliced
All the small bits of meat still on the carcass	Salt, pepper and allspice
1½–2 lb (700 g–1 kg) of sausage-meat	8 oz–1 lb (250–500 g) rashers of streaky bacon, thinly sliced

Note: If you are getting the butcher to bone the turkey, make sure he gives you the carcass and all the debris.

Prepare the stuffing by picking off all the meat still on the carcass. Mix it with the sausage-meat, sliced truffles, salt, pepper, allspice and the minced liver.

Spread the boned turkey body out, back down. Season the surface and cover it with alternate pieces of white and dark meat from the legs and wings of the turkey. Cover these with rashers of thinly sliced streaky bacon and finish with a layer of sausage-meat stuffing. Add a little more seasoning.

Roll up the stuffed bird and tie it securely to keep its shape during the lengthy cooking. (It now looks like a large sausage.)

Have ready a lidded casserole, large enough to take the galantine. Lay slices of streaky bacon in the bottom. Put in the galantine with enough water or stock to cover it, the chopped carrots, spiked onions, peppercorns, bouquet garni and seasoning. Cover and simmer for 3 hours.

When you judge it to be cooked, remove the galantine from the casserole and put it to cool in a terrine. The liquid will have reduced during cooking, reduce it further if necessary and then pour in the port. Put the galantine on a plate with a board weighted with 2½–4½ lb (1–2 kg) weights and leave for 48 hours.

Just before it solidifies and when the galantine is quite cold, pour the jelly over the meat and leave it to set in a cold place (*not* in a deep freeze).

Les Magrets de Canard Grillés
(Grilled duck breasts)

Time: 1 hour to marinade, 10 minutes a side to cook. Serves 4

4–6 breast of duck, according to size	Thyme and a bay leaf
1 glass of Armagnac	Salt and pepper

Score the skin of the duck breasts and put them into a terrine with the herbs and seasoning. Pour over the alcohol and leave to marinate for 1 hour.

When you are ready to cook them, take the breasts out of the marinade, put them under a hot grill and cook for 10 minutes or so each side. There should be enough fat in the duck for added fat to be unnecessary.

La Poule au Pot au Riz
(Boiled stuffed chicken with rice)

Time: 3 hours
Serves 6–8

4–5 lb (2–2.5 kg) chicken	12 pt (6 l) of water
8 oz (250 g) leeks, chopped	Salt and pepper
2 medium-sized onions, sliced	A bouquet garni
4 oz (125 g) carrots, chopped	

For the stuffing:

8 oz (250 g) sausage-meat	1 garlic clove, minced
6 oz (170 g) breadcrumbs	3 eggs, beaten
The chicken's liver, minced	Salt and pepper

To serve: a bed of rice and gherkins

Beat the eggs. Mince all the ingredients for the stuffing and bind with the eggs. Stuff the chicken and stitch the skin at the neck to hold in the stuffing. Put the vegetables, bouquet garni, the stuffed chicken and seasoning into a large pan with enough water to cover. Bring to the boil and skim. Leave to simmer for 3 hours.

When the chicken is cooked remove it, cut into joints and keep hot. Strain the liquid, reserving the vegetables.

To serve: *La Poule au Pot* can be served on rice that has been cooked in the strained liquid or it can be cooked in water and the bouillon can be served with vermicelli as a soup. Whichever method you choose, the vegetables are served around the chicken joints on the bed of rice, garnished with gherkins.

Les Cuisses de Coquelets Farcies
(Stuffed chicken legs)

Time: 30 minutes to prepare, 30 minutes to cook
Serves 4–6

8 chicken legs	1 liqueur glass eau-de-vie
2 oz (50 g) goose fat	1 tbsp plain flour
4 oz (125 g) large onions, sliced	6 rashers streaky bacon
1 oz (30 g) sugar	8 oz (250 g) small onions
1 oz (30 g) butter	6 oz (170 g) carrots, chopped
6 garlic cloves, crushed	Thyme and bay leaf
½ bottle of red wine preferably Cahors	3 lb (1.5 kg) potatoes, peeled

For the stuffing:

6 oz (170 g) ham	2 eggs
8 oz (250 g) sausage meat	10 juniper berries
8 oz (250 g) mushrooms	1 soupsp : Cognac
6 chicken livers	Salt and pepper

Beat the eggs. Mince all the stuffing ingredients, bind with the beaten eggs.

Bone the chicken legs. Fill the meat with the stuffing and roll each in a rasher of bacon. Tie them securely.

Heat the goose fat and brown the stuffed legs on all sides. Add the large onions, carrots and garlic. Leave to sweat for 5 minutes. Sprinkle in the flour, gradually stir in the ½ bottle of red wine and add the thyme, bay and eau-de-vie. Bring to the boil, cover and leave to simmer for 30 minutes.

Meanwhile, put the potatoes on to boil.

To cook the small onions: put them into a shallow pan with as much water as their height, the sugar and the butter. Cover with greaseproof paper and simmer until all the water has evaporated.

To serve: Arrange the chicken legs into a star on a serving dish. Beat the potatoes into a purée and alternate the purée with the little onions between the chicken legs. Strain the gravy and serve separately.

Le Cou d'Oie Farci
(Stuffed Goose's Neck)

Before the possibility of bottling or tinning, the stuffed neck was kept in a terrine, completely covered by the goose fat it had been cooked in. As the warm weather approached, the stuffed neck and its covering of fat was put to boil again for 5 or 10 minutes, and was then returned to a terrine to be kept for a further period under its protection of goose fat.

The neck can be served hot with haricots blanc and a sauce Perigueux or cold, sliced in small rounds.

A Pêcharmant goes very well with *Le Cou Farci*.

Time: 30 minutes to prepare and overnight to marinate, plus 1 hour's cooking

The skin from the goose's neck
2 lb (1 kg) goose or pork fat

For the stuffing:

1 lb (500 g) sausage meat	Salt, pepper and a pinch of
1 glass of Cognac	allspice
2 oz (50 g) truffle or truffle peelings	4 oz (125 g) of foie gras

This recipe can be made, as it is in Périgord, when you have bought a goose for roasting. Ask the butcher to skin the neck, though it is not difficult to do yourself. Care must be taken not to tear the skin, but you will find that it comes off easily.

Prepare the stuffing and leave it to stand overnight in a terrine for the ingredients to absorb the alcohol. Sew up the narrow end of the skin (the head end). Very carefully fill the skin with the stuffing, easing it evenly all the way down. When it is well filled sew up the open end.

Heat 2 lb (1 kg) goose or pork fat in a Le Creuset or similar cast-iron pan. When it boils, slide in the neck and allow to simmer for an hour (when it is cooked the neck will rise to the surface).

Drain, wipe and serve with haricots blancs and a sauce Périgueux (see p. 117).

Le Chapon à la Sarladaises
(The Sarlat capon)

Time: 20 minutes to the lb and 20 minutes over to cook; 8 days to hang
Serves 6

Mme Tuyot, La Grande Cuisinière of nearly 90, last cooked this dish for a wedding banquet in 1930. Some of the finest truffles grow in the Sarlat region, which probably accounts for the origins of this recipe, but with truffles presently reaching £300 per kilo in the Périgueux truffle market, some 'adjustments' to the suggested quantities may be thought necessary.

4–5 lb (2–2.5 kg) capon	The capon's liver
3 lb (1.5 kg) whole truffles	Truffle peelings
Salt and pepper	4 oz (125 g) streaky bacon

Wash, brush and peel the truffles (keep the peelings).

Make the stuffing by mincing the bacon, truffle peelings and the capon's liver.

Salt and pepper the inside of the bird and spread on a 'carpet' of the stuffing. Put in the whole truffles. *Fill* the inside with truffles, right into the crop of the bird, push them under the skin over the surface of the torso, sew up the neck skin. Leave the bird in a cool place for 24 hours.

Preheat the oven to 400°F, 200°C, Gas 6.

Roast the capon in the preheated oven according to its weight. A capon is a fat bird so no extra fat should be needed.

Les Confits
(Potted Meats)

A 'confit' is a way of keeping meat for a long time (as distinct from pâtés and terrines). It is a dish of high quality, unequalled by any other method of conserving meats. Because the meat is so rich, it is very economical, small portions satisfying both the appetite and the palate. It can be reheated gently or served cold.

Les Confits de Canard ou d'Oie Périgordins
(Traditional method)
(Périgord conserve of duck or goose)

The following is the method of preserving duck or goose meat which was used by Mme Tuyot's grandmother, and indeed everyone else, 150 years ago.

Time: Overnight standing plus 2 hours

1 goose or duck, whole	Fine salt and ground pepper
Fat cut away from entrails, finely chopped	Ground bayleaf
Fresh pork fat	Thyme

Leave the goose or duck to get quite cold after you've killed and plucked it. Remove the head and the pinions with a sharp knife. Make an insertion right to the breastbone and cut right along the length of the body. Pull away the flesh from both sides of the carcass – it comes away quite easily.

Cut the meat into four portions, each one having a leg or wing attached to the breast meat. Rub each quarter with a mixture of salt, pepper, bayleaf and thyme. (In the old days one also added a pinch of saltpetre to this mixture to help preserve the meat.)

Roll the pieces up and tie firmly with string. Put them into a terrine, well pressed up against one another, and leave them overnight.

Put the meat into a large pan in which you have melted all the grease that you have cut away from the entrails, plus some fresh pork fat if you don't think there is enough fat (there should be enough fat altogether to almost cover the pieces). Cook very gently for 2 hours. (Mme T's grandmother used to try sticking a straw into the flesh. If it bent, the confits weren't cooked enough. A skewer will do just as well if there is no straw to hand.)

Arrange the cooked confits in an earthenware dish or jar and pour over the strained fat. Cover with greaseproof paper and an air-tight lid.

This ancient method has the disadvantage that you will need to remove the confits before the beginning of summer to boil them up in their fat for 10 minutes before returning them to clean crocks or jars, or they may be spoilt by the heat.

Confit de Canard ou d'Oie (Modern method)
(Duck or goose conserve)

Nowadays one can buy the quarters of duck or goose ready cut from the carcass. Our Tuesday market is abnormally crowded at confit and foie gras season; the farmers' wives setting up trestles in the ancient covered market place to display their ready-prepared goose or duck quarters for you to make your own selection. (The carcasses are highly prized for *La Soupe* – a fact not fully appreciated by my daughter-in-law when she was living here. The shockwaves from her *refusal* of two carcasses in lieu of the francs owed for coaching a farmer's young son in English ('because we have no dog') have spread to the outer limits of the Périgord Noir.

Time: overnight standing plus 4 hours

Four quarters of duck or goose   Sea salt
1 lb (500 g) breast of pork

Having chosen your pieces of duck or goose meat, rub each piece with salt, place in a dish, cover, and leave in a cool place overnight.

Next day, cut up the pork into small dice and reduce *very, very* slowly (about 2 hours) over a very low heat. Wipe the excess salt from the duck or goose portions and place them in the 'melted' pork. Allow to simmer for 1½–2 hours. Remove the duck or goose pieces and arrange them in kilner jars (or litre tins, if you have the facilities for home tinning). Sterilize the jars or tins by boiling for 2½ hours or ¾ hour in a pressure cooker. Depending on the size of the pieces, no more than three can be fitted into a litre tin.

Le Confit de Dinde
(Preserved turkey)

Turkeys are available all the year round nowadays, but that is no good reason for not making a confit of the birds. In fact, frozen turkey gains in flavour from being 'confited'. The method is exactly the same as for the confit of duck or goose (see above). The results make the trouble well worthwhile.

Le Confit de Porc
(Pork conserves)

The importance of the pig in the life of Périgord has already been touched on in the section on pork. I say 'touched on' because it was but a glancing mention by comparison with the omnipresence of the animal both on and off the tables of Périgord. I am to some extent influenced myself by its presence, since all my scraps and vegetable peelings go towards the rearing of Mme Robert's cochons, but my presence will be remarked by its absence when *Le Saigneur* (the Bleeder) of the village sets in train the frenetic labour involved in processing the 140–200 kg of her pig. According to my First Edition Mrs Beeton, there were as many varieties of pig in Great Britain as there were shires, and, at the time of going to press, she estimated the pig population at 2 million. The black pig may be seen in Périgord, but the most 'common hog', as Mrs Beeton describes it, is the white pig, and a rough estimate of its numbers in the region may be based on the pig population of 60 in this commune of 257 persons. I am writing, of course, about *today's* pig population, of *today's* pâtés and conserves, and it is a remarkable fact that every traditional recipe for the cochon is still in production.

'Killing the Pig' is as much a communal activity as is the 'vendange' (see p. 176), and though the scene might inspire the brush of a Francis Bacon, there is almost an element of the picturesque about it. It appears that the pig's piercing cries have nothing to do with pain and everything to do with fear. What in its life has led it to expect to be strung up by its hind legs? An adroit Saigneur can kill a pig in a matter of seconds and it is in *everyone's* interests that he should do so, for even suspended by the hind legs a pig can be very dangerous. Each man and woman involved in this work has a definite role to play and from the moment that the pig's vermillion blood trickles into the cauldron with the vinegar in it to stop the blood congealing, the activity takes on a weird grace. People are seen at their best doing what they are best at, and though what they are best at is not attractive, their skill and certainty turns it into a ritual dance.

Close to nature, wrapped in nature, I see the unreality in citing recipes for *Le Confit d'Oreille de Cochon* (Conserved pig's ear), *Le Confit de Couennes* (Conserved pig's skin), *Les Andouilles du Carnaval* (Confit of the large intestine and the stomach) and *Les Boudins* (sausages made from the blood in that cauldron). The recipes are as legion as are the parts of the pig, but unless you live in the country, it may be difficult or impossible to procure the remoter parts of the animal, and so I am only citing the simple *Confit de Porc*: a conserve made from the best cuts. The recipe is straightforward, uncomplicated and, like other straightforward uncomplicated things in life, the results are very satisfying. With jars of *Le Confit de Porc* and *Les Grillons* in your larder, you will have the means to surprise and delight your family and friends.

Time: 48 hours standing, plus 2½ hours

4 lb (2 kg) fillet of pork	Sea salt
1 lb (500 g) larding pork	1–2 glasses water

Cut the pork into pieces each weighing about 8 oz (250 g) and tie them up like a parcel with strong string so that they don't alter shape during cooking. Rub the pork with plenty of sea salt and arrange in a terrine or earthenware dish. Leave for 48 hours in a cool place.

After 48 hours, rub off the excess salt. Cut the larding pork into dice and melt in a pan with the water. When the meat from the lardings has turned golden, put in the porc confit parcels and leave to cook over a moderate heat for 2½ hours. Arrange the meat in kilner jars and pour the fat over the top. Seal and sterilize in a pressure cooker for ¾ hour.

Les Grillons
(Potted meats)

Les grillons are not exactly what is meant by potted meat in Yorkshire, but it is very difficult to find a word to fit them. They are made from the residues from the confits, and are either a mixture of bits of duck, goose, turkey and pork meat from the lardings, or of pure pork from the Confit de Porc. *Les grillons* are immensely useful, both as a dish on their own and for making delicious stuffings (see stuffed tomatoes from Mme Robert, page 140).

Left-over meat from confit-making
Pepper
A few shallots, chopped

Left-over fat from confit-making
A little allspice
1 clove garlic, crushed

When you have been making confits, leave the remaining meat and fat to get cold. Make a seasoning of pepper (not salt, the residues will be salty), allspice, shallots and garlic and mix it into the debris from the confit-making. Reheat gently, turning as it warms, and put into smallish kilner jars. Melt the fat, pour it over the meat, seal and sterilize for ¾ hour in a pressure cooker.

LES SAUCES À LA MANIÈRE PÉRIGOURDINE

— The Périgordin Way with Sauces —

Other sauces than those given are in use in Périgord but their contents and the method of their preparation do not differ from the same sauces elsewhere in France.

La Sauce Périgueux
(Périgueux sauce)

Even the richness of the English language cannot supply a word to describe adequately this sauce when made to perfection. This recipe was given to me by one of the Grandes Cuisinières of Périgord and I treasure the scrap of paper she tore from an ancient exercise book to write it on. She is accustomed to cooking for large numbers, being in much demand for weddings and fête days, but here she has given me the quantities for 6–8 people.

If you like red meat, choose a fillet steak for this sauce. If you prefer veal, choose a joint. Either way, the meat is served with slivers of truffle on top and the sauce poured over. La Grande Cuisinière recommends a good Cahors Rouge to go with this glimpse of Heaven.

Time: about 35 minutes
Serves 6–8

12 oz (375 g) shallots, finely sliced ¼ bottle Madeira
1 heaped tbsp plain flour 2 lb (1 kg) cèpes, sliced
2 pt (1 l) chicken stock Salt and pepper
1 or 2 truffles, sliced Goose fat

Melt some goose fat and fry the shallots until they are deep golden in colour. Add the flour, sprinkling it over the shallots and gradually adding the chicken stock and half the Madeira, bit by bit. (This should make a rich, brown sauce.) Leave to simmer for 20 minutes.

Put the ingredients through a sieve or mouli (La Grande Cuisinière tells me that many people won't eat onions if they know they are there!) Add the cèpes, salt and pepper, and sliced truffles. Leave to simmer for a further 15 minutes. This sauce can be made the night before and gently reheated, adding the rest of the Madeira before serving.

Note: Some cooks replace the Madeira with dry white wine and eau-de-vie in this sauce. A glass of dry white wine and 1–2 tbsp of eau-de-vie are poured over the shallots and set alight while they are still frying. The recipe is in other ways unchanged, although of course it won't have the rich colour of the sauce with Madeira.

La Sauce au Vin Rouge
(Red wine sauce)

Time: 35 minutes

⅓ bottle good wine
6 medium-sized onions, finely sliced
2 tbsp goose fat
Salt and pepper
Bouquet garni

The white of 1 leek, sliced
1 rasher gammon or jambon de pays, minced
1 tbsp plain flour
2 garlic cloves, crushed

Pour the red wine into a small pan, heat rapidly and set alight. As soon as the blue flame begins to die down remove the pan from the heat.

Gently fry the onions and the white of one leek in goose fat. Add a spoonful of flour and allow to take colour.

Pour the flambéed wine into the sauce and add a bouquet garni. Leave to simmer at very low heat a little longer. Strain and reheat for serving.

La Sauce au Vin Blanc
(White wine sauce)

Time: 45 minutes

⅓ bottle good dry white wine (or half wine, half water)
4–6 oz (100–150 g) small white onions, finely sliced
Handful of shallots, chopped
A little goose fat or walnut oil

1 tbsp plain flour
Bouquet garni
1 pickled gherkin, sliced
Salt and pepper
A few sprigs parsley, chopped

Fry the white onions in a little goose fat or walnut oil. As they take colour, sprinkle a spoonful of flour over and add the liquid gradually. Season and add a handful of shallots and a bouquet garni. Leave to simmer for 40 minutes or so.

Just before serving, remove the bouquet garni and add the gherkin.

La Sauce Tomate
(Tomato sauce)

There is a saying in Pèrigord: 'the tomato is a famous cook', and once you have tasted tomato sauce in the manner of the Périgordines, you will appreciate the remark to the full. *'Las tomatas'*, as the tomato is called in the patois, is a prime vegetable of the region. The soil and the climate suit it to perfection and the Pèrigordines profit from this perfectly. The sauce is another example of their ability to marry ingredients, to balance the acid and the sweet, to retain nature's true clear colour. There is nothing insipid or anaemic about *La Sauce Tomate Périgourdine*!

Time: 45 minutes
Serves 6

6–8 large ripe tomatoes
4 small or 2 large onions, sliced
Goose fat
Salt and pepper
Bouquet garni (thyme, bay, parsley)

Chopped parsley or chervil to garnish
1 tbsp walnut or olive oil
1 shallot, chopped
1 garlic clove, chopped
A pinch of cayenne
A little stock or tepid water

Wash, wipe and cut the tomatoes into quarters. Remove the pips and squeeze some of the liquid from them. Heat a little goose fat and walnut or olive oil in a pan. Toss in the quartered tomatoes and the sliced onions, and cook them over a fast flame for 5 minutes, stirring with a wooden spoon. As soon as they have reduced a little, lower the heat, cover and simmer for 15 minutes *without water*. There is enough juice in the tomatoes to prevent them from burning. (This way of cooking the tomatoes has the dual advantage of reducing their acidity and maintaining their colour.) When the mixture is cooked, put it through a sieve.

In another pan, melt some goose fat and stir in the flour, gradually moistening the roux with a little tepid water or stock. Incorporate the sieved tomatoes and onions, the shallot and garlic, the bouquet garni and salt and pepper. Leave to simmer on a very low heat for 25–30 minutes. Just before serving, sprinkle with finely chopped parsley or chervil.

La Sauce à l'Oignon
(Onion sauce)

A popular sauce in Périgord. Their version differs from the classic recipe – neither milk nor cream are put into it, and it has the addition of minced ham or bacon.

Time: 30–40 minutes

Goose fat	Bouquet garni
8 oz (250 g) onions, finely sliced	Salt and pepper
4 oz (125 g) of ham or bacon, finely chopped or minced	A little stock or tepid water
	1 tbsp plain flour

Heat the goose fat and fry the onions and ham or bacon. As soon as they have a good colour, dust with the flour and stir in a little tepid water or stock. Put in the bouquet garni and season. Leave the sauce to simmer over a very low heat for 25–30 minutes.

To serve: Apart from taking out the bouquet garni, this sauce is served as it is, unstrained.

La Purèe à l'Oseille
(Sorrel purée)

Time: 30 minutes

1 lb (500 g) sorrel leaves	1 tbsp plain flour
1 tbsp goose fat	1 cup stock
A little chopped parsley and chervil	Salt and pepper

Wash, drain and wipe the sorrel leaves. Heat the goose fat and cook the sorrel for 5 minutes, turning with a wooden spoon.

Bring a saucepan of salted water to the boil and blanch the sorrel for 1 minute. Drain thoroughly.

When the leaves have reduced a little, sprinkle them with the flour and stir in the cup of stock. Season, add the chopped parsley and chervil, cover, and continue to cook *very* gently for 20 minutes.

Sorrel purée is served with veal and confit d'oie.

L'Aillade

This very Périgordin sauce is usually served with roast duck or roast hare. As will be seen from the preparation, it is another recipe for the enthusiast.

The blood of a duck or hare	3 garlic cloves, crushed
1 tbsp wine vinegar	Salt
The liver of the duck or hare	A pinch of cayenne pepper

Drain the blood of the animal into a dish containing a spoonful of wine vinegar.

Pound the liver, mix it with the blood and vinegar and put into a casserole with the garlic, salt and pepper. Leave to simmer over a very low heat and serve over the joints of duck or hare.

Le Verjus

It will be remarked that several recipes – particularly those for certain mushrooms – call for verjus. This is much used in Périgord in preference to lemon juice. It is simply the acid liquid pressed from unripe grapes. The juice is squeezed from the fruit by hand and then strained through a hair sieve. It can either be used immediately or bottled for such time as it may be called for.

La Sauce Moutarde
(Mustard dressing)

1 tbsp Dijon mustard	Salt and pepper
1 sherry glass walnut oil	

Thin the mustard with a glass of walnut oil, adding the oil drop by drop to ensure a homogeneous consistency. Add a pinch of salt and some pepper.

Note: This recipe can profit from the addition of a soft-boiled egg to the mustard.

La Mayonnaise Périgourdine
(Périgourdine mayonnaise)

This mayonnaise is made exactly as you would make an ordinary mayonnaise, but walnut oil is used, and you add a clove of garlic.

1 garlic clove   1 egg yolk
Salt and pepper   A touch of french mustard
Walnut oil   Vinegar
Chopped chives

Pound the garlic and mix it into an egg yolk. Add salt and pepper, and a minute touch of mustard. Turn the mixture with a fork *without* beating it, adding the walnut oil drop by drop. When the mayonnaise is sufficiently thick and plentiful, add the finishing touch with an *idea* of vinegar and some chopped chives.

Note: The trick to making this mayonnaise is to leave a little of the egg white attached to the egg yolk. This is an infallible, proven way of making a good mayonnaise.

LES LÉGUMES
— Vegetables —

Comprising:

Les Légumes (**Vegetables**)
Les Salades (**Salads**)
Les Fines Herbes et Condiments de Périgord (**Culinary Herbs and Condiments of Périgord**)
Les Champignons (**Mushrooms**)
Les Châtaignes (**Chestnuts**)

THE IMPORTANCE OF THE VEGETABLE IN OUR LIFE CANNOT BE OVERSTRESSED.

Rachel Carson's famous book *Silent Spring* predicted the present state of our environment, and Richard Mabey's *Food for Free* supported her call for sense and caution. Who cared? How many people listened? How many reflected that if our world became a wilderness there would be no voices to cry in it? Now, a third of a century later, the unease is spreading and even those who think that 'only Man is Vile' feel the need to help Nature to adjust the balance.

Some adjustments are in the nature of Nature, such as the growing rejection of antibiotics in favour of those remedies that don't impair the antibody, and the new old view of the true meaning of the quality of life. Twenty years ago, I sat in a cottage garden with friends, an open bottle of good Bordeaux breathing in the sunshine, eating sheep cheese from the Pyrenees, pain de campagne and a Ground Elder salad – and oh, life was good! The meal was simple, there wasn't a great deal of it, but it had such quality that we didn't *need* a great deal of it. It had sense and caution. Quality of life begins with health, and health begins with quality of food. We *are* what we eat, and the importance of the vegetable in our life cannot be overstressed.

The importance of the vegetable in Périgord was brought home to me, long before I undertook this collection of recipes, when I was called on to interpret for a foreigner who was suffering from acute diarrhoea. I might have brushed aside the six different vegetable remedies proposed by the six other patients in our doctor's waiting-room, but I could not ignore his written prescription for boiled carrot or rice water. The foreigner didn't ignore it, either – and it worked. I, my family and many Périgordins have also proved its efficacy (and if your children are suffering from 'tummy troubles', I recommend you to put carrots through a juice extractor, and give them the resulting liquid three times daily).

This incident was the dawning of my awareness that in Périgord the vegetable is not a mere palatable and colourful garnish to a dish. There is frequently a specific reason for its being served. Every discussion I have had or have overheard on vegetable cookery has included the therapeutic virtues of the vegetable in question, and because those virtues are germane to the use of these plants, as each vegetable makes its first appearance, the recipe will be preceded by a brief description of its merits.

I cannot begin, however, without reiterating my eulogy on the simple addition of pounded garlic and fresh parsley to French beans, runner beans, carrots and tomatoes. These vegetables, once cooked, are tossed in butter, garlic and parsley and served either with the meat or as a dish on their own – and are deliciously enhanced by the pounded juices of the 'hachis' of the garlic and parsley.

Les Légumes
(Vegetables)

LES BETTES OU BLEDES
(SWISS CHARD)

Swiss chard is not very well known outside the region. It is a visual cross between spinach and the outer parts of stick celery.

The leaf is cooked in the same way as spinach, sometimes with the addition of sorrel leaves, which suggests that it requires a 'lift'. The stalks are used in soups (and are a classic addition to pumpkin soup) or as a vegetable side-dish.

It contains vitamins A and C and is rich in iron. An infusion made from 30g of bette leaves in a litre of water taken 3 times a day is said to ease constipation and urinary infections.

Les Bettes à la Sauce Blanche
(Swiss chard in a white sauce)

Time: 30–40 minutes
Serves 4

2 lb (1 kg) of Swiss chard
1 tbsp plain flour
2 tbsp onion, finely chopped
Salt, pepper and a pinch of
    allspice
Goose fat or butter
1 egg yolk

A bouquet garni
A little tepid water
Garlic-rubbed fried croûtons
(Optional: Chopped gherkins or
    pickled nasturtium seeds as a
    garnish)

Separate the leaves from the stalks of the Swiss chard (reserve the leaves for another dish). Wash the stalks and cut them into 1-inch lengths. Throw them into boiling salted water and cook until tender. Test with a fork after 10 minutes. (Some cooks add a spoonful of flour to the water as it helps to keep the stalks white.) Drain and set aside to dry.

Heat the goose fat or butter and blend in the flour, moistening with the tepid water to a creamy consistency. Add the onion, seasoning, allspice and the bouquet garni. Leave to simmer, for 20 minutes. Put in the Swiss chard and continue cooking for 5 minutes or so. Beat the egg yolk with a little of the sauce and incorporate it into the pan. At this point the chopped gherkin or a handful of pickled nasturtium seeds can be added.

To serve: Remove the bouquet garni. Arrange the Swiss chard in a dish with a crown of garlic-rubbed fried croûtons around them.

LES CAROTTES
(CARROTS)

The carrot is one of our most valuable vegetables. In addition to numerous mineral salts, it is 7% iron and is consequently useful in maintaining red corpuscles and the haemoglobin count. It is also said to aid cell and tissue replacement. Since most of the goodness is in the skin, carrots should NEVER be peeled.

Among its virtues, too numerous to be mentioned in full, are its use for 'tummy troubles' as already cited in the preamble to this section, and the application of grated carrot and its juices to burns to prevent blistering.

Les Carottes aux Oignons
(Carrots with onions)

Time: 30 minutes

1–2 lb (500 g–1 kg) young carrots
6 oz (170 g) small white onions
A good knob of goose fat

4 oz (125 g) streaky bacon, finely chopped
Salt and pepper
Chopped parsley to garnish

Wash and top and tail, but *do not peel*, the carrots. If the onions you are using are not the small variety used in pickling, slice them finely.

Melt the goose fat, and cook the vegetables and the chopped bacon until they have taken on a golden colour, but are not brown. Season with salt and pepper, cover and leave them to finish cooking with only just enough heat under them to maintain the process.

When you are ready to serve, sprinkle them with chopped parsley.

LE CELERI
(CELERY)

Both the round and the stick celery have a stimulating action on the appetite. They are rich in vitamins A, B and C and contain sodium, phosphorus and potassium.

Beignets de Celeri-Rave
(Celeriac fritters)

Time: 30 minutes
Serves 4

Celeriac	½ oz (15 g) butter
4 oz (125 g) flour	1 egg
¼ pt (150 ml) milk	Pinch of salt

Sift the salt and flour. Add the well-broken egg. Beat until smooth. Melt the butter and stir it in. Add the milk gradually, beating all the time until the mixture is smooth. Let it stand for a while in a cool place.

Cut the celeriac into sticks of about 2 × ½ inch (5 cm × 1.2 cm). Dip the sticks in the batter and drop them into boiling oil. Drain on kitchen paper and serve dusted with fine salt and chopped parsley.

LE CHOU
(CABBAGE)

Cabbage has been referred to as 'The Medicine of The Poor', possibly because in arid regions of France it was almost all there was to live on. It contains vitamins A, B and C, minute quantities of arsenic (which are said to stimulate the appetite), phosphorus and potassium. Every variety of cabbage contains these properties, but red cabbage has them to a higher degree.

Le Chou Farci
(Stuffed cabbage)

Time: 3–4 hours cooking. Marinade overnight.
Serves 4

The importance of this famous dish to the French psyche and

stomach may be gauged by the number of old inn signs bearing its picture.

3 lb (1.5 kg) cabbage	12 oz (375 g) sausage-meat
6 oz (170 g) carrots, chopped	8 oz (250 g) breadcrumbs
4 oz (125 g) onions, sliced	5 eggs, beaten
4 ripe tomatoes, peeled	1 garlic clove, minced
A bouquet garni	Salt, pepper and allspice
4 rashers of streaky bacon	1 glass white wine
2 tbsp eau-de-vie/or Cognac	1 pt (575 ml) of water

Remove the coarse outer leaves of the cabbage. Trim away as much of the stalk as possible and cut out the heart, leaving enough good leaves to wrap the stuffing. Plunge the cabbage you are going to use into boiling salted water for 10 minutes to soften the leaves. Drain.

Make the stuffing with the sausage-meat, breadcrumbs, minced garlic, seasoning and allspice. Bind with the beaten eggs.

Put the stuffing into the centre of the cabbage and tie it into a secure ball. Stand it in a basin, pour over 2 tbsp of eau-de-vie or Cognac, turn it over once or twice and leave it overnight to marinate.

Heat some goose or pork fat and brown the cabbage all over. Remove it from the pan while you brown the carrots, onions and tomatoes in the same fat.

Lay some streaky bacon in the bottom of a casserole, put the cabbage on the bacon and arrange the vegetables around the cabbage. Season and add the bouquet garni. Pour over the water and white wine, cover and cook very gently for 3 to 4 hours, checking the liquid from time to time.

To serve: Remove the string from the cabbage and serve it on a hot platter surrounded by the vegetables. Take out the bouquet garni from the juices, degrease the liquid (allow to cool slightly and then skim), reheat and pour over the vegetables.

Le Chou Farci aux Châtaignes
(Cabbage stuffed with chestnuts)

Time: 1½ hours
Serves 4–6

1 large cabbage	1 pint (575 ml) of chicken stock
2 lb (1 kg) of shelled chestnuts	4 oz (125 g) carrots, sliced
3 oz (80 g) of goose fat	4 oz (125 g) onions, sliced
1 lb (500 g) of sausage-meat	5 garlic cloves
8 oz (250 g) of salt pork or salty	A bouquet garni
bacon	Salt and pepper

Remove the coarse outer leaves from the cabbage, detach the rest from the stalk and throw them into boiling water to soften them. Drain, run them through cold water and put them on a clean cloth. Cook the shelled chestnuts in the chicken stock for about 20 minutes. When cooked, remove them and keep the stock.

Mix the sausage-meat, chestnuts, salt and pepper and form into balls about the size of an egg. Wrap each in cabbage leaves and either put a piece of salt pork on each packet before you string them, or wrap each packet in a rasher of salt bacon and tie it securely.

Heat the goose fat in a casserole and cook the sliced carrots and onions for 5 to 10 minutes. Arrange the cabbage packets on top and pour in the chicken stock. Add the bouquet garni and the garlic cloves. Cover and cook over a low heat for about an hour (depending on the age of the cabbage).

To serve: Lift out the cabbage packets and put to keep hot, while you reduce and degrease the liquid a little (by cooling it slightly and then skimming it). Arrange the cabbage on the other vegetables and pour over the juices.

Le Chou-Rouge à la Périgourdine
(Red cabbage à la Périgourdine)

Time: 1–1½ hours
Serves 4

A large red cabbage   Goose fat
1 lb (500 g) uncooked chestnuts,   Salt and pepper
   peeled

Wash the cabbage and cut it into large portions. Put it into a casserole with the whole peeled chestnuts, a good knob of goose fat, salt and pepper.

Cover and allow to cook very slowly for at least an hour. As the cabbage is cooking in its own juices and the goose fat only it must be watched carefully, but this chore will be well rewarded by its delicious flavour.

LES FÈVES
(BROAD BEANS)

The broad bean has vitamins A, B and C, and dried broad beans make soups rich in iron.

Broad beans are most frequently made into a thick, garlicky soup, so frequently in fact, that the greengrocer dropped a head of garlic and a turnip into my basket when I bought a kilo of broad beans from his van (and didn't charge me for them).

Les Fèves en Ragoût
(Ragoût of broad beans)

Time: 30 minutes
Serves 4

2–3 lb (1–1.5 kg) broad beans	3 or 4 lettuce leaves
4 oz (125 g) small whole onions	Goose or pork fat
3 rashers of streaky bacon, chopped with parsley	Salt and pepper
	A little water

Shell the beans and remove their outer skins. Heat the goose fat and lightly cook the chopped bacon and parsley. Add the lettuce leaves, onions and beans. Season and pour in *very* little water. Cover, and leave to simmer over a very low heat for 20 minutes or so. By then, the water should have almost evaporated.

LES HARICOTS
(BEANS)

Les haricots verts, les haricots beurre, les mange-tout.
(French beans, yellow French beans, mangetout).

It is rumoured that the French bean was introduced into France by Catherine de Medici, but in fact it was brought from tropical America. The pods of all these beans are rich in phosphorus, potassium, iron and calcium.

The bean in all its forms appears frequently on the tables of Périgord. The haricot beurre is not our butter bean but a yellow variety of the French green bean. Our butter bean, known only by the general name 'haricot', is eaten both fresh or dried.

Les Haricots Frais à la Périgourdines
(Fresh butter beans à la Périgourdine)

Time: 1 hour
Serves 4

There are several varieties of these beans in Périgord, the Soisson being the choice of Mme Robert from whom I got this recipe.

Serve with chicken, pork or veal.

1 lb (500 g) ready-to-use fresh
   butter beans
Just enough boiling water to
   cover them.
1 onion, sliced

Salt and pepper
1 garlic clove crushed with
   parsley
A knob of goose fat or butter

Cook the beans in the boiling salted water, adding pepper and the onion. Cover and leave to cook for about an hour. Add a ladleful of water if you think necessary, but when the beans are ready to serve there should be no more than their own creamy liquid to moisten them.

To serve: Drop a knob of goose fat or butter into the beans, fork in the 'hachis' of garlic and parsley and pour over the juices from the chicken, pork or veal that will go excellently with the beans.

Note: Mme Robert's recipe differs from the traditional recipe. Traditionally, the knob of goose fat and the hachis of garlic and parsley are added to the beans halfway through the cooking time.

Les Haricots Frais à la Tomate
(Fresh butter beans with tomatoes)

Time: 50–60 minutes
Serves 6–8

2 lb (1 kg) ready-to-use fresh
   butter beans
2 pints (1 l) water
1 lb (500 g) whole tomatoes
1 large whole onion

A little fresh cream
1 garlic clove chopped with
   parsley
Parsley, chopped to garnish
Salt and pepper

Throw the beans into boiling salted water with the tomatoes and the onion. Reduce the heat and after 30 minutes add the 'hachis' of garlic and parsley. Continue to cook until the beans are ready and still unbroken. (The liquid should have been absorbed.) Bind with a little cream and serve sprinkled with chopped parsley.

Les Mange-Tout Jaunis
(Mangetout in sauce)

Time: 20 minutes
Serves 4

2 lb (1 kg) mangetout
2 medium-sized onions, sliced
1 tbsp plain flour
1 egg, separated

1 tbsp vinegar or verjuice
Goose fat
Salt and pepper
A little stock or water

Throw the mangetout into boiling salted water and cook for 5 minutes (they should be *'al dente'*). Drain and set aside. Heat the goose fat and fry the sliced onions until softened but not browned. Add in the mangetout, turning them briskly. Dust with the flour, moisten with a ladle of stock or water and leave to cook for 10 minutes or so. Just before serving mix the egg yolk with a little vinegar or verjuice. Toss the egg white over the mangetout and as soon as it has set take the pan from the heat and stir in the egg yolk.

Note: This recipe can be used for all varieties of green beans.

LES OIGNONS
(ONIONS)

The onion came into Europe from Egypt, where it was widely used in the preparations of early medicine. It is said to prolong life, a claim not easily proved but respected across the globe. In Bulgaria, where there is the highest number of centenarians in Europe, the onion is a national dish; in Berne, a whole week is devoted to the onion, every course (including puddings) being made with the vegetable; and a Mexican woman who lived to be 120 attributed her longevity to an almost exclusive diet of onions in infancy (she ate at least 4 onions at every meal).

Why is a bulb that brings tears to the eyes held in such high regard? Why do so many regions in France hold Onion Fairs but not Lettuce or Beetroot Fairs?

The Périgord is a wholehearted supporter of the Onion Cult. When M. Tonneau told me that he had never smelt cooking when passing *une maison anglaise*, he was really remarking that the onion is not ever-present around *my* doors and windows. Even in winter, with all doors and windows closed, an onion cloud hovers over the houses of Périgord and it is rare to find a man or woman without the smell of it on the breath. Certainly, there is a high tally of healthy 80- and

90-year-olds in the region – M. Fronsac (see 'The Waters of Périgord' p. 11) puts his continuing good health, if not his continuing presence in the world, down to a thrice-daily dose of grated raw onion and honey in a glass of good red wine, and though the uncharitable might say that people don't get close enough to him to pass on their germs, he may well have found the agreeably sure way to immunization. The onion has an astonishing number of virtues, but in order to profit from them fully it should be eaten raw – cooking destroys many of its active properties and it is for that reason that salads in Périgord are frequently garnished with a covering of grated raw onion.

Les Oignons Farcis
(Stuffed onions)

Time: 45–60 minutes
Serves 4

8 large onions, peeled	1 garlic clove crushed with fresh
1 lb (500 g) of sausage-meat or	parsley
minced left-over cold meat	Salt and pepper
6 oz (170 g) breadcrumbs	A little oil
1 or 2 beaten eggs	

Preheat the oven to 375°F, 190°C, Gas 5.

Cook the onions in boiling salted water for 15 minutes. Drain and leave them to go cold. Make a stuffing from the sausage-meat or cold minced meat, the garlic and parsley, breadcrumbs and seasoning and bind with an egg. Remove the heart of the onion, push in the stuffing and place the onion you removed from the centre on the top of the stuffing to form a lid or cap. (Alternatively, these pieces of onion may be added to the stuffing.)

Heat some oil and 'doré' the onions. Lift them carefully into an ovenproof dish, packing them close together to keep their shape during cooking and cook in the preheated oven for 40 minutes. The onions need to be golden and quite cooked for this dish to be at its best.

LES POIS
(PEAS)

In addition to vitamins A, B and C, peas contain iron, phosphorus and sugar. Locally, they are avoided by diabetics and persons subject to enteritis.

Les Petits Pois Périgordins
(Peas the Périgord way)

Serves 4

The dreary abundance of frozen peas puts many people off this vegetable. The following recipe for fresh peas could be adapted for frozen peas (with different timing) and should go some way towards reinstating them.

2 lb (1 kg) freshly shelled peas
4 oz (125 g) lean bacon, finely chopped
6 shallots, finely sliced

The heart of a lettuce
A sugar lump
Goose fat
Salt and pepper

Heat the goose fat in a casserole and fry the bacon and sliced shallots. Tip in the peas and 'doré' without allowing them to brown. (In fact, the peas take on a good green colour and a very good flavour.) Pour in a glass of water, add the lettuce heart, the seasoning and a lump of sugar. Cover and cook for about 20 minutes. The water should have evaporated, leaving the vegetables moistened by their own juices.

LES POMMES DE TERRE
(POTATOES)

Originally from the Southern Americas (the Incas called it the 'Patata'), the potato was carried across the Atlantic by the Spaniards and by the end of the sixteenth century was being used throughout Europe as animal feed. It was introduced to man's diet by Antoine Augustin Parmentier, pharmacist to the French Army in the reign of Louis XVI, who had come upon the vegetable in Germany. Despite the support of the King – support that earned Louis the title 'Enemy of the People', when the people learnt that the potato was a member of the plant family which includes belladonna – some years elapsed before Parmentier succeeded in bringing the vegetable to our tables. (It is a wise pharmacist who knows his own compatriots: Parmentier planted his potatoes on the outskirts of Paris and mounted an armed guard over them to excite the covetous instincts of the population – and we've been eating potatoes ever since. Parmentier went on to develop methods of cultivation and his efforts saved the population from starvation during the French Revolution.)

The potato contains 74.68% water, 22% carbohydrate and, depending on the quality of the potato, 5 g of potash. Thanks to M. Parmentier, the peoples of the world have devised 1,600 ways of cooking the vegetable, but though the potato has taken over from the chestnut in the nourishment of man and beast in Périgord, there are relatively few truly Périgourdin potato recipes. At the outset of my researches, because I came on so few local regional ways of cooking it, I naïvely supposed that a myriad of other wonderful things had pushed the potato to the back line of the chorus or even, perhaps, right off stage and I have been surprised and puzzled by the popularity of rather ordinary recipes. I have been almost as astonished by the diverse uses of the vegetable as I have by the diverse uses of wet bread (a particularly astonishing potato favourite being the potato omelette – even Mme Robert's *Omelette aux Pommes de Terre* is difficult to swallow), but in fairness to the great cooks of the region it must be emphasized that the least refined examples of 'diversity' are imports. The potato came to Périgord in the nineteenth century at a time when culinary influences from other regions were too insignificant to debase Périgourdin natural invention. The recipes they created *then* have become regional classics and the recipes that follow have been selected from their true taste of Périgord.

Les Pommes de Terre Confites

'Confites' as applied to potatoes is untranslatable. The nearest meaning is somewhere between 'baked' and 'sautéed'.

Time: 45 minutes
Serves 4

2 lb (1 kg) peeled potatoes, cut into rounds	2 garlic cloves chopped with fresh parsley
2 or 3 tbsp of goose fat	Salt and pepper

Have the oven ready, heated to 375° F, 190°C, Gas 5.

Cut the potatoes into rounds of ½–1 inch (1–2.5 cm) thickness. Peel the garlic, wash and dry the parsley and pound the two together in a pestle and mortar.

Heat the goose fat in an ovenproof casserole, put in the potatoes and brown them over a quick flame, turning them all the time. Season and add the garlic and parsley 'hachis'. Cover and put into the preheated oven. Leave to cook for 30–35 minutes turning them over every 10 minutes.

To serve: Drain the potatoes on to a hot dish and serve at once.

Les Pommes de Terre à la Graisse d'Oie
(Potatoes cooked in goose fat)

You may be thinking 'so what?', but there *is* a difference. When a goose is being roasted place it on a trivet (or the rack from your grill pan). Cut the potatoes in halves and lay them in the bottom of the roasting dish and put the trivet and goose above them. All the juices and richness from the goose drip on to the potatoes and give them an exquisite flavour. (I would not say that this is a uniquely Périgourdin method of cooking. See reference to the cooking of beef in Yorkshire, p. 78.

Les Pommes de Terre à la Sarladaise
(Potatoes from Sarlat)

Time: 35 minutes
Serves 6

3 lb (1.5 kg) potatoes, thinly sliced
1½ lb (700 g) cèpes, sliced
4 oz (125 g) truffles, sliced

6 oz (170 g) goose fat
2 garlic cloves chopped with fresh parsley
Salt and pepper

You will need 2 separate frying pans.

Wash and slice the cèpes and rid them of their moisture by warming them in a little heated goose fat. Take them out, clean the pan and heat some fresh goose fat in it. Return the cèpes to the pan and allow them to cook slowly.

In the other pan, heat the rest of the goose fat and put the sliced potatoes to cook in it for about 20 minutes.

Ten minutes before the end of the cooking time add the cèpes and the sliced truffles to the potatoes and leave them to cook together for a further 10 minutes.

To serve: Arrange the vegetables on a hot dish and garnish with an 'hachis' of garlic and parsley.

Ragoût de Pommes de Terre
(Potato ragout)

Time: 30 minutes
Serves 4

2 lb (1 kg) potatoes, peeled and
    cut into largish pieces
A 'hachis' of garlic and parsley
4 rashers of streaky bacon,
    chopped

2 large onions, finely sliced
Goose fat
Stock
Salt and pepper

Lightly brown the potatoes in the goose fat, add the chopped bacon and finely sliced onion. Season and continue to cook for another 5 minutes. Pour in enough stock to reach the top of the ingredients without completely covering them. Put on a lid and finish the cooking over a low flame for about 20 minutes.

To serve: Strain and garnish with the 'hachis' of garlic and parsley.

Terrine de Pommes de Terre Truffes
(Terrine of potatoes with truffles)

Time: 1½ hours
Serves 4

2 lb (1 kg) potatoes
1 large glass of white wine
1 truffle

4 oz (125 g) gammon, minced
1 tbsp goose fat
Salt and pepper

Peel and slice the potatoes. Heat the goose fat and stir in the minced gammon without allowing it to brown. Slice the unpeeled truffle and lay it in the bottom of an ovenproof dish, put in the potatoes and sprinkle the minced gammon over them. Season and pour in the white wine. Cover and leave to cook slowly for 1½ hours.

LE SALSIFI
(SALSIFY)

This nourishing vegetable derives from the scorzonera (see p. 39) and is rich in minerals. Like Jerusalem artichokes, salsify contains a certain amount of insulin.

La Tourtière de Salsifi
(Salsify pie)

Time: 2–3 hours to 'rest' the pastry, 2 hours to cook the pie
Serves 10

This extraordinary dish – a wonderful Périgourdine creation – is traditionally made with 2 young chickens and 3 lb (1.5 kg) of salsifi, but the birds may be replaced by 3 lb of lean gammon, pork or veal (or, though the flavour won't be as good, by precooked chickens).

La Tourtière au Salsifi is one of the dishes that was included in the menu at a wedding, the pastry case often reaching huge dimensions. The first time Mme Peyreac (from whom I got the recipe) saw the dish, it was carried in state to the bride – and when the lid was removed half a dozen live chickens were revealed in the coils of the turban. The tourtière was subsequently taken away and filled with its proper ingredients. A tourtière is often cooked when the pig has been killed, the filling then being made from pork rather than poultry.

Note: You will need a very large, deep pie dish.

For the pastry:
1 lb (500 g) plain flour
2 eggs
Salt and pepper

8 oz (250 g) lard
1 egg yolk, beaten
A little water

For the filling:
2 young chickens of 3 lb (1.5 kg) each
1 tbsp flour
Stock
3 onions, finely chopped

Salt and pepper
3 lb (1.5 kg) salsify
1 garlic clove, chopped
A little vinegar

To make the pastry: pour the flour into a large basin and make a hollow in the centre. Beat the 2 whole eggs, melt the lard and pour them into the hollow. Sprinkle with seasoning and mix the paste rapidly with the fingertips. Flour a board, form the paste into a ball and leave it to 'repose' for 2 to 3 hours wrapped in a cloth.

To make the filling: bone the chickens and make a good stock with the carcasses. Scrape the salsify, cut it into 1–2 inch (2.5–5 cm) lengths and leave it to stand in water with a little vinegar added to keep it a good colour.

Heat the goose fat and brown the chicken flesh. Add the onions, the garlic and the seasoning. Dry the salsify and add it to the other ingredients. Sprinkle a tablespoon of flour over them and gradually stir in enough stock until the contents are three-quarters covered. Put on a lid and leave to simmer for an hour.

To prepare the pie crust (which will be baked 'blind'): preheat the oven to 400°F, 200°C, Gas 6.

Divide the pastry into 2 portions, one-third and two-thirds. Roll out the larger portion to cover the bottom of your dish, leaving a good overhang, and either place a well-greased plate on to the pastry base or twist a clean tea-towel into a turban and arrange it on the pastry. Roll out the smaller piece of pastry and place it over the greased plate or tea-towel turban, bringing up the overhang to join the lid. Pinch the two together at 4 places only around the circumference. Glaze with the egg yolk and cook in the preheated oven for 15–20 minutes.

To serve: carefully separate the pie lid from the base using a very sharp knife and take out the plate or 'turban'. Lift the chicken and salsify mixture into the pie base, pour over the reduced juices and replace the lid of the pie. Serve at once.

LES TOMATES
(TOMATOES)

The tomato has Peruvian origins and was brought to Europe by the Spaniards in the sixteenth century. Curiously, it is considered to be a great revitalizer. I say 'curiously' because of its close culinary links with the onion, whose revitalizing properties have already been extolled. The links between these two vegetables make me marvel. In a sense, to marvel is to question. Sometimes, of course, one marvels with acceptance, but there are many marvels in Périgord that raise questions in my mind. How is it, for example, that scientifically untrained countrymen do exactly as they scientifically should in the cultivation of say, the truffle? (See Mushroom section, p. 155.) Mme Robert has no degree in chemical reactions – yet she *knows* that, chemically, tomatoes and onions are perfectly balanced. Such little miracles and marvels occur daily that it would not astonish me to discover that I had been chemically seduced into making my home in Périgord by the 'parfum' of tomatoes and onions being cooked together in Mme Robert's kitchen behind the post-office. *Did* some aromatic substance lay a spell on me and impregnate my brain with a Revitalizing Faith?

Well, as I said of the onion, marvels are difficult to prove. It is difficult to prove that it is the onion that has made one live so long (or the lack of it that cuts one off in one's prime). The cure you believe in is the cure that does you the most good. Let me encourage you to enjoy the tomato to the full. Not only is it refreshing (i.e. *revitalizing*) in summer (being 90% water) but it contains vitamins A, B, C and K.

Les Tomates Farcies
(Stuffed tomatoes)

Serves 4

This is Mme Robert's superb recipe for a simple dish that may be enriched by the inclusion of pâté de foie gras and yet remain reasonable in price. A marvellous dinner party dish.

Serve with rounds of toasted bread that have been well-rubbed with garlic.

8 large tomatoes (2 per person)

For the stuffing:
8 oz (250 g) pâté, sausage-meat or
    left-over cold meat, minced
4–6 oz (125–170 g) breadcrumbs
4 oz (125 g) shallots, chopped
    finely

1 egg
Salt, pepper and parsley
A little eau-de-vie (optional)

For the sauce:

8 oz (250 g) onions, sliced finely   8 oz (250 g) tomatoes, skinned
Goose fat   and cut up
                                                              Salt and pepper

Choose large firm tomatoes, allowing however many you feel
appropriate (2 per person is usually enough if the stuffing is very
rich). Remove the stalk/leaf end. Turn the tomatoes over and cut out
a cap from the underside. Remove the inside of the tomato carefully
with a teaspoon, keeping all the bits you cut out. Make a stuffing with
either some confit de porc, pâté de foie gras or any left-over meat. Mix
the meat of your choice with breadcrumbs, some finely chopped
shallots, salt, pepper and parsley, and bind with an egg. Fill the
tomatoes with the mixture, dip each in flour and fry them gently
stuffing downwards first then turn them and fry on bottom edge. (If
wished a little eau-de-vie may be added to the stuffing.)

Arrange the tomatoes carefully in an ovenproof dish, placing them
close together so that they keep whole during cooking. Cook in a
moderate oven (350°F, 180°C, Gas 4) for 15 minutes.

While the tomatoes are cooking, put the onions in a pressure
cooker. When almost cooked turn them into a frying pan and *doré*
them in butter or goose fat. Skin the tomatoes for the sauce by
dropping them into hot water for a minute or two. Chop them, and
add them to the frying pan. Cook until soft, then mouli the contents
of the frying pan. Pound some garlic and parsley in a mortar and add
to the puréed sauce. Pour the sauce carefully into the oven dish
letting it ooze round the tomatoes rather than go over them.

Allow to cook a few minutes longer and then serve on rounds of
toasted bread that have been well-rubbed with garlic. (The
combination of tomatoes and onions is perfection itself, the one
balancing the acidity of the other.)

Note: I had completed this recipe, and the stuffed tomatoes were in
the oven when a neighbour arrived with a plastic bag heavy with
wonderful vegetables fresh from her garden. She asked me what
meat I was using in the stuffing. 'The left-overs from a guinea-fowl,' I
told her. 'That won't do at all,' she said firmly. 'The guinea-fowl is too
insipid to go with tomatoes.' Well, there they were, cooking away in
the oven! This incident demonstrates the hyper-sensuality of the
French taste buds, but I *liked* the stuffing.

LES TOPINAMBOURS
(JERUSALEM ARTICHOKES)

Many people are surprised to learn that the nutritional value of the Jerusalem Artichoke is superior to that of the potato. It contains abundant quantities of vitamins A and C and is rich in carbohydrate, albumen and vegetable fats. Its distinctive flavour, similar to that of the heart of the globe artichoke, limits its links with other ingredients and it is perhaps for that reason that M. Parmentier elected to champion the potato.

Les Topinambours en Beignets
(Jerusalem Artichoke Fritters)

In Périgord there are many recipes for fritters – les beignets. Here is one for Jerusalem artichokes:

Batter (see p. 169)

Peel the artichokes and cook for 15 minutes in salted boiling water. Drain, and leave to go cold. Cut them in smallish rounds, toss in batter and fry in hot oil for 5 minutes. Drain and serve sprinkled with salt, pepper and chopped parsley.

Les Salades
(Salads)

Salads are particularly appreciated in Périgord and neither the midday meal nor supper would be complete without a bowl of fresh greenery coming to the table. At midday the salad is eaten from the plate that has served for the meat and at supper, always a light meal (perhaps soup, omelette, salad and fruit), it may be served from the omelette plate or even, at more simple suppers, from the soup bowl after Le Chabrol (*see* Soups, p. 21).

The manner of making a dressing varies almost from house to house. Many cooks have their own favourite recipe ready made up, an old wine bottle of the 'house blend' always to hand on the dresser, but chez Mme Tuyot dressing the salad is an impressive ritual. As soon as the meat plates are empty a tray containing a salad bowl, condiments, fresh herbs and a little wooden cup and rod, worn smooth with use, is placed before the old lady. The size of the bowl depends on the number of people at the table, of course, but whatever its size, the bowl is always exactly three-quarters full of whichever salad is to be eaten that day. Mme Tuyot is over eighty but long practice has made perfect the dexterity and certainty with which she measures and mixes her ingredients. Her left hand holds the little wooden cup while her right drops in pinches of salt, pepper and herbs. A trickle of vinegar or verjuice is added and the contents of the cup are agitated with the wooden rod to dissolve the salt before it reaches the lettuce leaves. The refinement of this ritual lies in the notion that the salad can only absorb the aromatic ingredients *before* the oil is added, since once the leaves are coated in oil they will not be able to take up the other flavours of a dressing. Mme Tuyot's dance routine never varies: 1 part verjuice or vinegar is sprinkled over the salad, followed by the contents of her little wooden cup, followed by 2 parts walnut or olive oil and her performance ends with a cheerful flourish of the salad servers. My own taste-buds are not sufficiently refined to distinguish between Mme Tuyot's method of 'fatiguing' a salad, as it is called, and a salad dressed with the same ingredients previously mixed but I would lay odds that Mme Tuyot would triumph in a blindfold test.

Salads made from endive, dandelion or chicory are served with *Les Chapons d'Aillés*. *Les chapons* are pieces of bread lightly rubbed with crushed garlic and tossed into the salad just before it is 'fatigued'.

Note: (For those who find the flavour of walnut oil too strong for a simple green salad.) Walnut oil may be mixed with other oils in the following proportions: One-third walnut oil to two-thirds peanut oil. As with olive oil, the quality and flavour of walnut oil depends on several factors – age and method of pressing, for example. A few finely chopped walnuts make a delicious addition to a salad, even if you are not using walnut oil in the dressing.

LA SALADES DES CHAMPS
(SALADS FROM UNCULTIVATED EDIBLE PLANTS)

Salads picked from the fields and hedgerows are both aromatic and nourishing – and apart from being the property of the owner of the ground, they are free. All salads picked from the wild should stand in vinegar and water for a while before the business of washing them begins in earnest (the vinegar releases the worms, etc.). The plants most commonly used in these salads are cresson (cress), mâche or la doucette (corn salad or lamb's lettuce), pissenlit (dandelion), pourpier (purslane) and scorsonère (black or wild salsify).

Cresson
(Cress)

Watercress is one of the finest edible plants of our hemisphere. In the days when street venders 'cried' their wares it was advertised as 'La Santé du Corps' (Health for the Body). It was commercially grown in England as long ago as the eighteenth century – and the cultivated plant has exactly the same virtues as the wild variety; iron, phosphorus, sulphur, iodine, calcium and vitamins A, B and C.

Salade de Cresson
(Cress salad)

All green stuffs to be eaten raw must be washed very thoroughly. Begin by standing the cress in water to which a little vinegar has been added. After 30 minutes or so, lift out the cress, throw away the water and vinegar and wash the cress in several changes of water. Spin dry and serve very simply with a little salt (no pepper required) and chopped walnuts.

La Mâche or La Doucette
(Corn salad or Lamb's lettuce)

A light, refreshing salad (now grown commercially in France), rich in vitamin C. It is said to help one sleep. To prepare as a salad, follow the cleaning procedure given for cress (see above).

Serve with a dressing made of 1 part lemon juice or verjuice, 3 parts walnut or olive oil. A little chopped garlic may be added.

Le Pissenlit
(Dandelion)

During my researches into the properties of the dandelion I was surprised to learn that, because the flowers open at break of day and close at dusk, the plant has ravished as many poets as botanists. It was a sentence packed with new information. I was born and bred in the country yet I have never noticed that the dandelion opens at dawn and closes at dusk. Furthermore, searching my memory and several anthologies of English poetry, I have found no poet so ravished by the dandelion that he wrote on it. Perhaps the poets who did were French, though the word and the meaning of the word 'pissenlit' is far less ravishing than the word and the meaning of the word 'dandelion'.

The dandelion contains vitamins A, B and C, iron, magnesium and calcium. It is said to be undeniably diuretic, but though (after cress) it is my favourite salad, I have never noticed such an effect.

Other than dressed very simply, in Mme Tuyot's fashion (with or without the addition of *Les chapons*), the following recipe is the local way with the dandelion.

La Salade de Pissenlit Périgourdine
(Périgord Dandelion Salad)

Serves 4

1 lb (500 g) of washed dandelion leaves	Oil, vinegar, salt, pepper and mustard
4 oz (125 g) streaky bacon, cut small	A little chopped garlic (optional)

Wash and drain the dandelion leaves. Put the salt, pepper, vinegar and a little mustard into the bottom of a large salad bowl. Throw in the leaves. Heat the oil and fry the chopped bacon. Add the oil and the bacon to the salad bowl, toss well and serve at once.

Le Pourpier
(Purslane)

I would be unable to identify English purslane, a variety found only on salt marshes and similar maritime areas. No such areas exist in Périgord, which suggests that the plants may not be identical. It grows here on stretches of open, uncultivated ground. Mme Robert makes a point of sowing it in her vegetable garden and one or two commercial growers have taken up its cultivation. The fleshy leaves have a nutty flavour and they make a refreshing salad.

La Salade de Pourpier aux Œufs Durs
(Purslane salad with hard-boiled eggs)

A good handful of purslane per person	Pepper
1 hard-boiled egg per person	1 tbsp of lemon or verjuice
Sea salt	Red peppers chopped in rounds
	3 tbsp walnut or olive oil

Sprinkle the purslane with sea salt and leave it to stand for 4 hours.

Have ready the hard-boiled eggs. Rinse and drain the purslane. Put the juice, oil, chopped red peppers and pepper (no salt) into a large salad bowl. Put in the purslane, cut the eggs into quarters and add to the salad. Mix thoroughly, taking care not to damage the eggs.

La Scorsonère
(Black or wild salsify or scorzonera)

Scorzonera has all the same virtues as the larger variety of salsify but it is the buds of scorzonera that are most often used in Périgord (see Omelettes p. 37).

Pick the buds just before they open into flower and add them to either a cultivated or wild salad.

LES SALADES DU POTAGER
(SALADS FROM THE VEGETABLE GARDEN)

La Salade Périgourdine aux Endives
(Périgord chicory salad)

Serves 6

Without laying blame at anyone's door, Endive (French) is Chicory (English) while Chicorée (French) is Endive (English).

12 oz (375 g) of chicory	1 tbsp mustard
6 oz (170 g) of smoked Jambon du Pay (or pre-cooked smoked gammon)	3 hard-boiled eggs
	3 oz (80 g) Gruyère, diced
Walnut or olive oil	Vinegar
	Salt and pepper

Note: Jambon du Pays is raw; it may be successfully replaced by cold cooked smoked gammon.

Wash, drain and dry the chicory (the leaves may be left whole and separated or chopped in rounds). Dice the ham and the Gruyère. Using 1 part vinegar to 3 parts oil, make a vinaigrette incorporating the mustard, salt and pepper. Tip into a large salad bowl, add the chicory, ham and cheese, turn about briskly, garnish with sliced hard-boiled eggs and serve at once.

La Salade des Gésiers d'Oie
(Goose gizzard salad)

Goose gizzards can be bought tinned or frozen in France; if you have no possibility of acquiring them, poultry livers can be tried in their stead.

Serves 6

12 oz (375 g) endive	1 tbsp mustard
6 goose gizzards	Walnut or olive oil
Salt and pepper	Vinegar
Goose fat	

Wash and drain the endive. Slice the gizzards and fry them in the goose fat. Make the dressing with the mustard, oil, vinegar and seasoning and pour it into the bottom of a large salad bowl. Toss in the salad and the hot goose gizzards, turn about briskly and serve at once.

La Salade aux Truffes
(Truffle salad)

Serves 4

If you grow lettuce – *never* throw away the tops when it begins to sprout; it is at this moment that the lettuce contains the greatest therapeutic properties, such as an increase in the vitamin E content.

The white wine in this recipe may be used instead of vinegar in the dressing.

A lettuce big enough for 4	Chopped parsley and chervil
A small tin of truffles (4–8 oz, 125–250 g)	8 oz (250 g) cooked potatoes
3 tbsp of walnut or olive oil	2 tbsp of dry white wine
	Salt and pepper

Drain the truffles from the tin and heat without boiling in the white wine. Allow to go cold.

Prepare a dressing with the wine, oil and condiments. Chop the parsley and chervil finely. Cut the cold cooked potatoes into small rounds and mix the chopped herbs into them. Pour the dressing into a salad bowl, put in the potatoes, herbs and prepared lettuce. Slice the truffles into the other ingredients, turn the salad thoroughly in the wine dressing and serve at once.

La Salade de Riz aux Truffes
(Rice Salad with Truffles)

Rice is frequently used in salads in Périgord – a dish of rice, fish and cold summer vegetables make a refreshing supper on those suffocating evenings in August when man and nature *long* for that storm to break.

Apart from vitamins A, B1 and B2, rice contains vegetable fats, carbohydrate, calcium, iron, iodine and fluoride.

Cultivated or wild, black or red, radishes contain the same properties, though in different degrees. They contain vitamins B and C, iodine, magnesium, phosphorus and sulphur.

To say, merely, that the olive contains vitamin C and is rich notably in potassium may seem to dismiss it lightly – but what more needs to be said about the olive than that it is a tree that merits our reverence?

Here the three are combined in a delightful salad.

8 oz (250 g) cooked rice for 4 people	1 small tin of truffles (4–8 oz, 125–250 g)
4 oz (125 g) of green olives	2 oz (50 g) of Gruyère
2 hard-boiled eggs	Salt, pepper and parsley
Walnut or olive oil	The juice of a lemon
4 oz (125 g) of radishes	

Cut the olives, radishes and cheese into small pieces. Drain the liquid from the truffles and wipe them. When dry, slice the truffles and add them to the other chopped ingredients. Mix them thoroughly with the cooked cold rice. Pour over the dressing made from 1 part lemon juice to 3 parts oil, with salt and pepper added. Once the salad has taken up the flavour of the dressing, serve garnished with hard-boiled eggs cut into rounds and chopped parsley.

La Salade aux Capucines
(Nasturtium salad)

Nasturtium has been in medical and culinary use for centuries. The properties to be found in extracts of essential oils serve in both chemical and herbal pharmaceutical preparations. Much use is made of pickled nasturtium seeds in Périgord, particularly to replace capers in a recipe.

This salad is dressed only with nasturtium flowers and it is one of the most refreshing, cleansing salads of the region.

Separate the leaves of a good-hearted lettuce and wash them. Drain and toss into a large salad bowl. Cover the surface with a layer of nasturtium flowers, turn the salad over and over and serve at once. You will find that the lettuce has been 'seasoned' by the flowers.

LES FINES HERBES ET CONDIMENTS DE PÉRIGORD
(THE CULINARY HERBS AND CONDIMENTS OF PÉRIGORD)

Apart from the truffle and the walnut, none of the plants listed here can be specifically linked with the Périgord – they are linked in the heading to the section because of the part they play in the life and cuisine of the region. Plants, too, *are* what they eat and the benefits of the Périgord's fertile soil serve plant and man alike.

There is still an immense amount of work to be done on the nutritional and therapeutic properties of the world's vegetation – our environment deserves our respect; the minerals taken up by the roots and the vitamins that abound in plant tissue are essential to the body's continuing health. Where the virtues of any herb or condiment are either in doubt or not known to me only the culinary advantages will be mentioned. Herbs are cultivated from the wild to intensify their flavour rather than to produce Bigger and Better plants and until I learnt this basic fact I was surprised by the quantity of wild herbs used in La Cuisine Périgourdine. *If you are using wild herbs you will need twice the quantity needed of the cultivated variety.*

L'Ail
(Garlic)

The first visual record of garlic (*c.* 4500 BC) is thought to be that on one of the three pyramids at Gizah from which it was learnt that the pharaoh Cheops had a daily ration of the condiment distributed to his workers to give them strength and protection from epidemics.

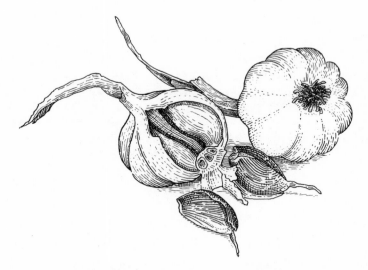

This almost divine belief in the protective and healing properties of garlic has continued down the centuries. During the outbreak of the Plague in 1726, four Marseilles burglars who were making a 'safe' living by pillaging the houses of the dead, are said to have attributed their immunity to the intake of immense amounts of garlic soaked in other ingredients – a preparation now known as 'The Antiseptic Vinegar of the Four Thieves'. (History doesn't relate how this history became history, but it looks as if the Antiseptic Vinegar won't give immunity from the Law). There are still corners of Europe and the world where garlic is strung round the necks of babies and infants – as it was in ancient Egypt – to protect them from worms and evil spirits.

Gastronomically, garlic is reputed to aid digestion, a claim I have heard even from die-hard sceptics. The disadvantage of the condiment, particularly to the city dweller, is obvious. There are one or two recipes for deodorizing the breath, but in the French countryside, where everyone is eating garlic, it doesn't matter how strongly you smell.

Le Basilic
(Basil)

The two varieties of basil in common use are sweet basil and wild basil. Both are rich in essential oils and are said to have a soothing effect gastrically. The herb has been in use in the kitchen and in medicine since the twelfth century. In Périgord both varieties are added into the 'bouquet garni' or are chopped finely to garnish sauces and mushroom dishes.

Le Cerfeuil
(Chervil)

Chervil was used by monks in the Middle Ages in the preparation of potions for helping the circulation. It is a herb whose active properties are totally lost as it dries and it should not be picked until just before needed. As it frequently re-sprouts after the flowering season (though the second growth has no flowers), it can be picked almost all the year round. A wonderfully versatile herb, it can be used in salads, chopped as a garnish or added to hot dishes.

La Ciboulette
(Chives)

[Many people think that 'fines herbes' is the French for chives, but 'fines herbes' has the equivalent meaning to our word herbs.]

Chives are another adaptable plant, equally good in a salad, as a garnish or in a hot dish. It has the added virtue of giving one the taste of onion without making one smell of onion.

Le Fenouil
(Fennel)

Fennel grows almost everywhere in the world and is universally respected for its medicinal and culinary properties. Infusions made from fennel can help eliminate catarrh and soothe the upper respiratory tract. Richard Mabey tells us in *Food for Free* that fennel was one of the Anglo-Saxon 9 sacred herbs. Every part of the plant is edible.

Le Genièvre
(Juniper)

The fruits or berries of the juniper are used in both the kitchen and in medicine. The shrub is rich in essential oils and apart from the pharmaceutical extraction of its properties, home preparations of ointments and soothing baths are made for the relief of rheumatism. The shrub is also used in veterinary medicines. The berries are frequently used in the kitchen in Périgord, as will be seen from several of the recipes in this book. The wood of the shrub is sometimes used in the smoking of hams.

Le Laurier
(Bay)

At the outset of my researches into the therapeutic properties of plants (working alphabetically in English), I was brought to a discouraging halt by the paucity of information on the bay. I had supposed that the plant's merits had been brought to a head, as it were, in the symbolism of a Crown of Laurel, but perhaps there is nothing more to that use of the plant than that it keeps its shape and its leaves live longer than most. Its use in the 'bouquet garni' (which one removes before serving a dish) is widespread throughout France, but the only instance I have come across of bay leaves being actually masticated came from a very old lady of the region. She attributed her strong teeth and healthy gums to munching several bay leaves each morning.

La Noix
(Walnut)

The importance of the walnut in the daily life of Périgord would surprise even Frenchmen from other regions. The Dordogne is France's principal producer of the walnut, over 2,000 walnut plantations and some 170,000 isolated trees yielding between 7 and 12 thousand tons yearly.

The sight of men, women and children bending and crawling under pouring rain in the accumulation of that tonnage is almost as distressing as the labour itself. (I have given the nut harvest serious thought – why not, for example, stretch nets larger than the diameter and circumference of the tree? – but to voice my thoughts would be trespass.) The tree's commercial value is the cause of many bitter wrangles in court when the land on which it stands is to be rented, or to change hands by sale or inheritance.

Sodden clothes, aching backs, blackened hands and legal squabbling are only the negative aspects of the walnut's importance, however. Its positive benefits are vitamins A, B and (while still green) powerful quantities of vitamin C. It is 50% oil and has an astonishingly high calorie count per pound. It also contains phosphorus, iron and lime.

The best quality walnut in Périgord (growing mainly in the Thiviers, Thenon, Exideuil and Terrasson areas) is the 'Corne'. I don't like walnuts, even when they are cracked for me to cleanse the palate before tasting a wine, as is the custom in Périgord, but *les Cornes* have gone a long way towards changing my opinion.

L'Olive
(Olive)

See comments prefacing *La Salade de Riz*, p. 148.

L'Oseille
(Sorrel)

The Périgordines make good use of sorrel, particularly when eggs are on the menu (see, for example, L'Omelette à l'Oseille, p. 42). It is said to help digest hard-boiled eggs (which, one is told, require as much energy as they supply to be digested). Many precook sorrel for a minute or two before adding it to a dish, thus reducing the rather acid flavour of the leaves.

Le Persil
(Parsley)

I was encougaed – *made* – to eat quantities of parsley as a child because it was said to have more vitamin C than any other green plant.

Parsley has been known and respected for centuries, every part of the plant, root, leaf and seed being used medicinally. In addition to high quantities of vitamin C, the herb contains vitamin A, iron, lime, calcium and phosphorus. It is no wonder that the herb is so abundantly used throughout the world.

Le Roumerin
(Rosemary)

Rosemary contains essential oils that stimulate the flow of gastric secretions, bile and urine. It is used in ointments and liniments to ease rheumatic pains.

Le Sauge
(Sage)

The therapeutic virtues of sage resound in its very name; its Latin name means 'to save' or 'to cure', whilst *we* call it 'wise'.

Infusions made from ½ oz (15 g) of leaves per litre of water are used here to soothe coughs and disorders of the upper respiratory tract. It is also said to have a cleansing, disinfecting effect (which may account for our use of the herb in stuffings to be served with pork). The plant's essential oils, which vary in strength depending on where the plant is growing, are used in medical preparations and though I have said less about this herb than about garlic, were I able to plant only one or the other, sage would be the plant of my choice.

La Truffe
(The Truffle)

In the Périgueux 1989 truffle market, the truffle reached a price of £300 per kilo, but the truffle's rarity and consequent price is not the only reason for the sobriquet 'Black Diamond'. Most people regard the truffle as a means to 'perfume' a dish, but there are growers who believe it contains untapped *nutritional* riches. The word 'aphrodisiac' has an element of the superficial or the ridiculous about it, but it is a fact that the smell of the truffle gives a pig an erection. Other animals such as deer, foxes and boars are similarly affected by the truffle's smell. The growers, who are neither superficial nor ridiculous, do not suggest the truffle is an aphrodisiac to man. They do suggest that it has other energizing properties, however. It is difficult to understand why such a famous condiment should have been overlooked by nutritional chemists and though scientists at Toulouse have succeeded in reproducing the truffle's aroma synthetically, their researches would appear to have financial rather than nutritional value.

The truffle grows underground and is found on the roots of certain trees growing in poor soil. In France, the principal tree species are the hazel, the hornbeam and the oak, the *quercus ilex* in particular. (In Britain beech trees have been found to yield truffles). The interrelation of the tree under stress, struggling to make its way in adverse conditions, and the succouring development of the fungus would be worth investigating, even if we didn't want to eat the fungus, and certain truffle-growers have been putting 'two and two together' in an attempt to save the mushroom from extinction.

Until relatively recently, little grain was grown in Périgord and, because litter was expensive, farmers went into the woods and coppices to sweep up fallen leaves and gather dried bracken and undergrowth for litter. In areas where the soil was already poor, gathering this potential compost deprived it even further. Remembering his grandfather's use of leaves, one grower 'stressed' a number of his trees whose truffle crop had declined in recent years, by blowing the fallen leaves away with a mechanical blower. Knowing that the heavy seasonal rains (April and August) were as necessary to the truffle's development as the stress of the tree, he compensated for recent droughts by watering the ground during those periods and the result of these operations was an excellent crop of truffles.

It is difficult to know whether the mystique surrounding the truffle is due to the 'unknowns' (a mini-mystique by comparison with the How the Universe Began mystique, but with a grain of that same awe), to its commercial value, or to a deep respect and trust in its health-giving properties. The mystique, awe and reverence are there – and one is touched by a shiver of it even if that tiny slice of truffle on top of the pâté de foie gras makes little impression on the palate.

LES CHAMPIGNONS
(MUSHROOMS)

There are over 300 species of edible fungi and mushrooms growing in Périgord and it may not be possible for those reared on the fully-stacked shelves stretching away into the hypermarket distances to appreciate the influence they exert on this community. For centuries, the mushroom has been known in the region as 'The Poor Man's Meat' and even 50 years ago it was an essential source of protein. Centuries of hardship cannot be sloughed off in a matter of 50 years, if indeed ever, and the collective respect for the mushroom is undiminished – though perhaps it is now more a Passion than a Protein.

Hunting for mushrooms is not merely 'an enthusiasm'. Something out of the ordinary happens in Périgord at mushroom seasons. An indefinable atmosphere, almost as marvellous as the magic spores themselves, permeates the region. People become uncharacteristically secretive. They slip furtively from their houses as dawn breaks – earlier and earlier – as the mania takes a hold. They become 'distant', offhand, offensive – and, finally, utterly exhausted by the hunt and the arduous toil of cleaning, cooking and conserving kilos and kilos of mushrooms.

The depth of the passion has necessitated official intervention; people die every year through a mixture of gluttony and ignorance, and strenuous efforts are being made to impress on the public the serious consequences of *not* knowing your mushrooms. Very comprehensive leaflets are handed out in pharmacies and hospitals as mushroom fever gains epidemic proportions. Posters appear in public buildings giving advice on what to wear and how to equip yourself for the hunt – the woods and forests of Périgord abound with vipers. Fortunately for the medical profession, the 300 or so mushroom varieties don't all develop at the same moment, spring, summer and autumn having their respective harvest – and in winter the wondrous 'Black Diamond' of Pèrigord, the truffle, comes to perfection.

The truffle and cèpe are the 'vedettes' of mushroom cookery in Périgord. They have inspired the creation of many dishes and sauces. None of the other mushrooms in common use in La Cuisine Périgour-dine have had recipes specifically created for their enhancement and apart from being used in omelettes, are usually treated very simply. The recipes on pp. 156–62 are examples of ways in which most other varieties of mushroom are cooked, and they are suitable for all the mushrooms mentioned, though a particular mushroom may be named in the recipe title.

The varieties most commonly used in Périgord are girolles (the chanterelle), the morille (morrel), the oronge (royal agaric or Cesar's mushroom), the rosée (the mushroom most commonly found in fields in Britain), les trompettes des morts, les Catalans and les coucourles or filleules (English varieties, if any, unknown to me).

Les Truffes
(Truffles)

See pp. 147–8 for truffle salads.

La Truffe à la Croque du Sel
(Raw truffles with salt)

A simple and delicious way of eating truffles.

Scrub and rinse the truffles – but don't let them stand in the water. Dry them and eat as radishes, dipped in salt.

La Truffe Farcie
(Stuffed truffles)

Time: 15–20 minutes
Serves 4

6 oz (170 g) cèpes, chopped	A little flour
6 oz (170 g) gammon bacon, minced	1–2 glasses of port
Goose fat	1 glass of white wine
	Salt and pepper

Preheat the oven to 400°F, 200°C, Gas 6.

Brush and wash the truffles. Cut them in half and carefully scoop out the centres. Mix together the truffle centres, the chopped cèpes and the minced gammon. Make a 'roux' with a little flour and goose fat and moisten with some of the port. Add this into the mixture of truffle centres, cèpes and gammon and stuff the emptied truffle halves with the mixture. Arrange the truffles in an ovenproof dish, pour in the remaining port and white wine to the level of the stuffing, bring the liquid to boiling point and put the dish in the oven for 15–20 minutes.

Les Truffes à la Perigourdine
(Truffles à la Périgourdine)

Time: 35–40 minutes
Serves 4

4 truffles	15 fl. oz (425 ml) Madeira
6 oz (170 g) foie gras	Salt and pepper
8 oz (250 g) plain flour	Goose fat
6 oz (170 g) butter	Sauce Périgueux (see p. 117)
4 oz (125 g) sliced onions	

Preheat the oven to 450°F, 230°C, Gas 8.

Make the puff pastry in the usual way, finally dividing it into 4 portions.

While the pastry is being made, heat the goose fat and *'doré'* the sliced onions. Add the whole truffles and leave them to sweat for 5 minutes. Pour in the Madeira, season and allow to simmer for 20 minutes. Lift out the truffles, drain and leave to go cold.

When the pastry has had its final roll and has been divided into 4 equal portions, wrap each truffle in some foie gras and enclose in a pastry envelope. Cook for 15 minutes in a very hot oven.

Serve hot, accompanied by a Sauce Périgueux made from the liquid in which you have cooked the truffles.

Les Truffes au Vin Blanc
(Truffles in white wine)

Time: 20 minutes

This method of cooking truffles serves either when they are to be a side-dish to poultry or when they are to be eaten on their own.

Clean the truffles and put them in a casserole. Sprinkle with salt and cover with a good white dessert wine with a high degree of alcohol. Cook without boiling for 20 minutes. Drain and serve as a side-dish or on their own.

Les Cèpes
(Cèpes)

The notice on the door of the post-office announcing that it was closed for a month and the tense little group (including the postman and two gendarmes) bent over the open boot of Mme Robert's car was all I needed to know that cèpe-hunting had begun. The year before Mme Robert had conserved *67 kilos* of cèpes – and that is all you need to know to know that she is a mushroom-hunter par excellence. Finding cèpes is not as straightforward as finding other sorts of mushroom. It is not just a question of catching sight of one while you are out for a walk in the woods and the official advice to wear stout shoes and thick socks and to carry a stick is sound advice. A book published in Périgord between the two world wars describes mushroom-hunting as 'a very healthy passion', the author going on to claim that every child of 8 upwards could tell a good from a bad mushroom and that it is only elsewhere in France that one hears of cases of poisoning. Whether or not that was true then, it is not true today, and the extent of Mme Robert's skill and knowledge in finding 67 kilos of edible boletus is brought home to one at every seasonal fatality.

See also: L'Omelette aux Cèpes (p. 38) and recipes for cèpes cooked in the roasting tin under poultry or game birds (pp. 99–111).

Les Cèpes Farcis à la Périgourdines
(Stuffed cèpes)

Time: 40 minutes
Serves 6

12 medium sized fresh young
   cèpes
Walnut or olive oil
6 sliced shallots
8 oz (250 g) salty bacon, minced
6 oz (170 g) breadcrumbs
2 oz (50 g) butter

Toasted breadcrumbs for garnish
4 garlic cloves, sliced
1 garlic clove, crushed
Fresh parsley
4 tbsp milk
Salt and pepper

Wipe the cèpes (but don't wash them). Separate the heads from the stalks and chop the stalks finely. Wash, drain and chop a good bunch of fresh parsley (you should have 2 heaped tablespoons).

Soak the breadcrumbs in the milk, squeezing out the excess. Heat the oil and gently fry the minced bacon, the shallots and the chopped cèpe stalks. Mix these into the breadcrumbs and add the 4 chopped cloves of garlic and the parsley. Season to taste.

Rub the inner surfaces of an ovenproof dish with the crushed garlic and trickle a little oil over the base. Heat the oven to 425°F, 220°C, Gas 7. Garnish each cèpe head with the stuffing and arrange them in the ovenproof dish. Sprinkle the tops with the toasted breadcrumbs and put a knob of butter on each. Put into the preheated oven and cook for about 25 minutes.

Serve immediately in the dish they were cooked in.

Les Cèpes aux Pommes de Terre
(Cèpes and potatoes)

Time: 35 minutes

Equal quantities of cèpes (sliced)
   and potatoes (chopped)
Walnut or olive oil

A good handful of chopped
   parsley
Salt and pepper
1 garlic clove, crushed

Heat the oil and fry the sliced cèpes and chopped potatoes until uniformly golden. Season with the salt and pepper, sprinkle the parsley and garlic over them, cover and cook gently for 30 minutes or so.

Les Cèpes en Terrine
(Cèpe casserole)

Time: 2 hours
Serves 6

12 medium-sized fresh cèpes
12 oz (375 g) gammon bacon,
    minced
2 beaten eggs
4 shallots, chopped
Salt, pepper, parsley and
    tarragon

6 oz (170 g) streaky bacon,
    minced
4 oz (125 g) breadcrumbs
1 large onion, chopped
2 garlic cloves, chopped
Goose fat and walnut oil
Tomato sauce (see p. 119)

Preheat the oven to 375°F, 190°C, Gas 5.

Clean the cèpes without letting them stand in the water. Separate the heads from the stalks and chop the stalks finely. Make a stuffing from the minced gammon, streaky bacon, breadcrumbs, the chopped onions, shallots and garlic, the parsley, tarragon, salt and pepper, and bind it with the two beaten eggs.

Put a tablespoon of melted goose fat and a tablespoon of walnut oil into a terrine or ovenproof dish. Starting with a layer of stuffing, fill the dish with alternate layers of stuffing and cèpes ending with a layer of cèpes. Cover with foil or a lid and cook for about 2 hours in a moderate oven.

Have ready a tomato sauce and serve the cèpes with the sauce poured over or as a separate garnish.

Les Morilles au Verjus
(Morrels in verjuice)

The stalk of this mushroom has no culinary value.

Time: 30 minutes

Having removed the stalks, wash the heads in vinegar and water. Dry on a clean cloth. Heat some oil in a casserole, slice the mushrooms and toss into the hot oil. When they have taken on a good colour, sprinkle with salt and pepper, cover and cook gently for 30 minutes.

To serve: Garnish with chopped parsley and a trickle of verjuice. Garlic-rubbed fried croûtons go well with these mushrooms.

Les Girolles à la Persillade
(Chanterelles seasoned with herbs and ham)

Time: 30 minutes
Serves 4

1 lb (500 g) of chanterelles
8 oz (250 g) gammon bacon,
 minced
A handful of fresh parsley,
 · chopped

Salt and pepper
1 garlic clove, chopped
2 tomatoes, skinned and seeded
Walnut or olive oil
Verjuice or vinegar

Remove the stalks from the chanterelles and wash the heads in vinegar and water. Have ready a saucepan of boiling, salted water – drop the mushroom heads into the water and allow them to 'blanch' for 5 minutes. Drain and dry on a clean cloth.

Heat the oil and brown the mushrooms. Mix together the minced gammon, chopped garlic and parsley, add the mixture to the chanterelles, season, cover, and leave to cook for 30 minutes.

Just before serving trickle over the verjuice or vinegar. Alternatively, instead of the verjuice or vinegar, two skinned and seeded tomatoes may be added to the pan at the same moment as the 'persillade'.

Les Oronges Grillés
(Grilled royal agaric)

This mushroom is highly prized in Périgord, some gourmets preferring it to the cèpe. It is usually found in groups of two or three on edges of woods or ditches, but it is rare. There are several varieties within the species growing in Britain, but in general they are said to be rather tasteless. Perhaps this member of the family is 'Royal' because it is equally well appreciated in Britain as in Périgord.

This method of cooking mushrooms is used throughout Périgord for all field mushrooms, but most particularly for the 'oronge', a tender, delicately flavoured mushroom. The grilling can be done under a grill or over a charcoal fire.

Remove the stalks, wash the heads and dry them on a clean cloth. Brush the mushrooms with oil. Cook them for a few minutes under the grill. Then turn them over to cook the other side.

Serve with an 'hachis' of shallots, parsley, salt and pepper and a little verjuice, vinegar or lemon.

Les Coucourles or Filleules Grillées

I have not traced an English translation of these names, which suggests that the mushroom doesn't grow in Britain. It may well be available from British greengrocers and markets, however.

The information on the coucourle came to me from a fellow traveller on a Périgord branch line. He was returning home after a day of mushroom-hunting and he was pleased to show me the contents of his basket (*never* a plastic bag for mushrooms). He described the coucourle as 'a fine, upright mushroom, with a large pointed cap, with an underside of pink folds or pleats'. Only the cap is eaten – and 'a most exquisite delicacy is achieved by brushing them with oil and passing them over the cinders of a wood fire. A flip of salt (I describe my companion's actions), a psst of lemon – *et voilà!* A dish fit for La Rème d'Angleterre!

LES CHATAIGNES
(CHESTNUTS)

Man's place in nature and nature's place in man could be symbolized by the chestnut tree. Before men began to neglect and destroy their environment this tree was respected and valued. In summer it gave shade to sheep and cattle, in autumn its fruits fed man and beast and in winter its fallen leaves gave warmth and comfort in the stable. The wood of the tree makes fine floors or can be burnt in a range – it isn't the wood for an open fire as it spits out burning particles.

The chestnut's importance in man's diet is emphasized by the existence of a special cast-iron chestnut pot (*L'Oule*) and of the X-shaped wooden implement (the *Ruffadou* or *Escouradour*) for removing the chestnut's inner skin. The pot is pear-shaped and lidded and it stands in the hot embers on three stout legs.

Like the walnut, the Périgord chestnut is of superb quality and it keeps well. To store the nut, it would first be soaked in water for a couple of days to release the worms, after which it would be dried on racks or by regular turning, as is the way with the walnut. The autumn air of Périgord is full of the swoosh swoosh swoosh of nuts being turned – but none of the charm or romanticism that the idle onlooker may derive from this activity touches M. Tonneau's stony heart. M. Tonneau's view of the chestnut is influenced by the autumn evenings of his childhood, evenings spent with the family ranged on benches at the long kitchen table, each member with his allotted pile of chestnuts to peel. M. Tonneau's grandmother would spread a clean cloth down the centre of the table for the peeled nuts and she kept a sharp lookout for bad workmanship. It was hard enough, having spent the afternoon gathering the nuts, to spend the evening shelling them – but worst of all, M. Tonneau told me, 'It took the surprise out of next day's lunch'.

The first recipe here is a dish that Mme Robert ate as a child. Her parents were very poor and her mother must have had a hard time trying to feed four children. Nevertheless, despite having been reared on an almost meatless diet, chestnuts, mushrooms and walnuts taking the place of meat, Mme Robert is a tall woman with an excellent figure. The dish is very good – and even better when reheated next day. As with so many things in Périgord, it improves with keeping.

Mme Robert's Chestnut Meal

Time: 30–40 minutes to cook
Serves 4

2 lb (1 kg) of shelled chestnuts	Salt and pepper
1 lb (500 g) sliced potatoes	A little water
A small turnip, sliced	Parsley to garnish

In M. Tonneau's household vine leaves lined the bottom of the pot, which added a little 'quelquechose' to the flavour of the chestnuts. [If you do not have a proper pot (see p. 162) use a Le Creuset or similar casserole]. When a pear-shaped pot was used, no water would be added.

The worst thing about chestnuts is getting the two skins off. Remove the outer skin with a knife, then boil some water and toss in the chestnuts. Boil until you see the inner skin is splitting. Remove the pan from the heat. Do not strain. Peel off the inner skin while still in the hot water – you will get burnt, of course …

Line the bottom of a casserole with the sliced turnips. Add a layer of sliced potatoes. Finish with the whole peeled chestnuts. Season and add a very little water, just enough to prevent the turnips from sticking to the bottom. Cover and cook very gently until tender for 30–40 minutes. If you have a kitchen range, so much the better. The regular heat all over the bottom surface of the casserole gives the best results.

Châtaignes Braissées
(Braised chestnuts)

Time: 40–60 minutes

24 chestnuts, peeled   A little goose fat or bouillon
Red wine sauce (see p. 118)

Place some peeled chestnuts in a casserole large enough for them to lie separately. Make a red wine sauce (see relevant section) adding a little Madeira. [There should be enough liquid to cover the chestnuts by about ¼ inch (0.5 cm).] Place in an oven slow enough to maintain gentle simmering for 45 to 60 minutes (not more than 350°F, 180°C, Gas 4). Make sure the sauce doesn't dry up, adding a little goose fat or bouillon if necessary. Serve glazed by the sauce, turning each chestnut about to ensure that it is well covered. This method goes well with game birds.

Les Crépinettes à la Périgourdine

Time: 20 minutes to cook the chestnuts, 10–15 minutes to grill the crépinettes
Serves 4

Crépinettes are generally a small flat sausage made from finely minced pork wrapped in caul. The Périgordines have their own version of the crépinettes, always a winter dish because they are made when the pig is killed and when truffles and chestnuts are available. This version is *Les Crépinettes aux Châtaignes*.

2 lb (1 kg) sausage-meat   Chopped thyme
1 lb (500 g) shelled chestnuts or   2 garlic cloves, chopped
    unsweetened tinned chestnuts   Salt and pepper
Stock to cook the fresh chestnuts   A little Cognac
Goose fat   Caul
Breadcrumbs

Remove the outer shells of the fresh chestnuts with a sharp knife and cook the chestnuts in the stock for 20 minutes. Mix together the sausage-meat and chopped garlic and thyme, seasoning and a little Cognac. When the chestnuts are drained and cool, wrap each in sausage-meat. Wrap the sausage balls in caul, dip them in melted goose fat, roll in the breadcrumbs and grill under a medium grill, turning frequently.

See also *Le Chou Farci aux Châtaignes* (p. 128) and *Le Chou-Rouge à la Périgourdine* (p. 129).

LES FROMAGES
—— Cheeses ——

Visitors to Périgord are often disappointed by the absence of regional cheeses. The reason for this lack is simple: the geography of the region doesn't allow for large-scale dairy-farming. In this commune, typical of hundreds of others in the Départment, a herd of 30 cows is seen as 'important' and it is not surprising, therefore, that cheeses have not caught the inventive interest of the Périgordines. Goat and cow cheeses are made throughout Périgord, but they are home-made for home consumption, or, when there is a milk surplus, to be sold from a little table in the local market. The cheeses are made no differently in Périgord than anywhere else in the world (including a London flat, if you so wish). The most celebrated goat cheeses come from the Thiviers area, while Saint-Marcelin is known for cheeses of mixed goat and sheep milk. The fabrication of these cheeses depends on a milk surplus and they have a fairly limited life. It is still usual to keep a cow, just as it is still usual to keep a pig, and once the grass has begun to sprout (round about Shrove Tuesday), I know the moment has come for me to knock on Mme Benoit's door with my plate, damp cloth and 10–franc piece for one of her cheeses.

The range of puddings in Périgord is curiously limited. This may be due to a combination of abundant seasonal fruits and the superb work done by the Périgordines in bottling and freezing these fruits for winter consumption.

The first three recipes were given to me by Mme Tuyot our local Grande Cuisinière, and even she was hard put to it to think of a *Périgourdine* pudding.

Les Macarons
(Macaroons)

Time: 30 minutes

Both walnuts and hazelnuts are to be found everywhere in Périgord – walnuts, of course, are a main crop of the region – and these macaroons can be made with either nut.

8 oz (250 g) pounded nuts   4 egg whites
8 oz (250 g) castor sugar

Heat oven to 300°F, 150°C, Gas 2.

Pound the nuts in a large mortar with a little sugar to absorb the oils that would be otherwise lost. Beat the whites of 4 eggs to a very stiff consistency, work the castor sugar into the egg whites and add to the nuts. Put spoonfuls of the mixture on to oiled paper and cook them for 20–30 minutes in a slow oven.

Les Merveilles Périgourdines
(Périgordin Marvels)

Time: 10–15 mins (approx.)
Serves 4

8 oz (250 g) plain flour   A few drops of lemon essence
A pinch of salt   1 tumbler of tepid water or cold
½ tbsp castor sugar   milk
2 eggs beaten together   1 oz (30 g) butter, melted
1 liqueur glass of eau-de-vie or   ¼ oz (5.5 g) yeast
   rum   Vanilla sugar for dusting

Mix together the flour, salt and sugar. Make a dip in the flour and pour in the beaten eggs, the glass of eau-de-vie or rum and the lemon essence. Add the melted butter and the yeast to the liquids in the dip and gradually incorporate the flour into these ingredients, adding the tepid water or milk as you do so. The resulting paste should be thick enough to roll out easily. Roll out the paste and cut it into smallish squares. Taking care not to cut through the pieces, mark each with a criss-cross pattern. Heat some oil to boiling in a deep fryer. Drop in the *Merveilles* and as they swell and brown turn them over to cook on the other side. Drain onto a hot dish and garnish with vanilla sugar. (It is impossible to give an exact time for the *Merveilles* to cook: it is best to drop in a 'tester' before you begin.)

Note: If you have interesting pastry shapers, this adds delight to children.

Les Beignets
(Fritters)

1 lb (500 g) flour	A little eau-de-vie or rum
1 tsp fine salt	Sugar
hot water	Chopped walnuts
6 eggs	

Make a fritter batter by adding hot water little by little to the flour and salt to form a dough. Beat 2 eggs and work them into the dough. Repeat this twice, adding 2 beaten eggs each time. The batter should then be of a consistency to remain on an upturned spoon. Moisten that batter with eau-de-vie or rum. Heat oil in a deep-fryer and drop in spoonfuls of the mixture, about 4 or 5 at a time. Drain them on to a clean cloth and serve sprinkled with sugar and chopped walnuts.

Beignets de Cérises
(Cherry fritters)

This is an unusual way with fresh cherries.

Make a fritter batter (see above recipe). Keeping groups of cherries on their stalks, dip them into the batter and then into hot oil. It's fun but it does require dedication.

Le Clafoutis

Time: 45 minutes

The clafoutis is a sort of toad-in-the-hole but with fruit in the batter rather than sausage. It is really a Limousin pudding, and is generally made in that region with black cherries. In Périgord it is made with any fruit in season that cooks well. It is eaten hot or cold – or lukewarm, even.

A good handful of cherries or a dozen greengages
4 beaten eggs
4 glasses of flour
4 glasses of castor sugar

Pinch of salt
2 tsp eau-de-vie
As much milk as necessary to form a thick consistency

Mix all ingredients except fruit to make a thick batter. Butter a baking tin whose sides are about 2 inches (5 cm) deep. Arrange the fruit of your choice to fill the bottom of the baking tin and pour over the batter. Cook in a moderate oven (350°F, 180°C, Gas 4) for 45 minutes.
  Serve sprinkled with sugar.

L'Omelette Flambée

Serves 6

10 eggs
6 oz (170 g) castor sugar
Salt

Butter to cook the omelette
Eau-de-vie or Cognac

Beat together the eggs, sugar and salt. Heat the butter and make the omelette in the usual way. Heat a good glass of eau-de-vie or Cognac, set it alight, put the omelette on to a heated serving dish and pour over the alcohol.

Le Massepain de Périgord
(Périgord Marzipan)

Time: Approximately 1 hour
Serves 6

This must be the only marzipan in the world that doesn't have almonds in it. It is really a very light biscuit which, if all has gone well, may rise to 2 or 3 inches (5 to 7.5 cm). (There is a saying in Périgord that cakes don't like to be looked at too often.) This 'marzipan' makes a useful base for several sorts of pudding, either served hot or cold, whole – or split and filled with raspberries, strawberries, walnuts, chestnut purée – what you will.

10 eggs	1 packet of yeast (11 g)
8 oz (250 g) of sugar	1 packet of vanilla sugar (7.5 g)
8 oz (250 g) of plain flour	A little orange-flower water
1 oz (30 g) of butter	

Preheat the oven to 350°F, 180°C, Gas 4.

Sieve the flour. Separate the whites and yolks of the eggs. Beat the yolks, the vanilla sugar, the sugar and the orange-flower water and gradually stir in the sifted flour. Beat the whites to stiff points and gently incorporate into the other ingredients.

Grease and flour a baking tin, put in the mixture and cook in a moderate oven for about 1 hour.

Serve hot, sprinkled with sugar, or split when cold and garnish with the filling of your choice. A particularly delicious summer pudding can be made by sprinkling the two halves with eau-de-vie and joining them together with stiffly beaten cream, raspberries and finely chopped walnuts.

Mme Robert's Tarte aux Pommes

Fruit tarts are popular in Périgord, either made with a flan or pastry base, Mme Robert's apple tart is sprinkled with eau-de-vie and coated with finely chopped walnuts before going into the oven.

Time: 30–40 minutes
Serves 4

8 oz (250 g) peeled and cored sweetish eating-apples	garnish when cooked
4 oz (125 g) shelled, chopped walnuts	8 oz (250 g) plain flour
	A good pinch of salt
1 tbsp Cognac, Calvados or eau-de-vie	4 oz (125 g) margarine or lard
	1 tbsp castor sugar
A sprinkling of vanilla sugar as	Very cold water to mix

Sieve together the salt and flour and stir in the sugar. Rub in the fat to the consistency of fine breadcrumbs. Add cold water very gradually until you have a soft dough. Roll out on a floured board. Cover the base of a tart tin with the pastry and cut the apples finely, arranging them in a pleasing design. *Make sure there are plenty of apples.* Cover with the chopped walnuts and trickle over the Cognac, Calvados or eau-de-vie. Trim off the overhang of pastry and bake in a hot oven

(450°F, 210°C, Gas 7 for 30–40 minutes. Just before serving, sprinkle with vanilla sugar. (Do not put the sugar on top before the tart goes in the oven as you will ruin the flavour of the vanilla.)

Summer Compôtes

At least an hour before serving, sprinkle raspberries or strawberries with sugar and 2 glasses of good red wine.

Peaches can also be served in this refreshing way; slice the peaches, sprinkle them with sugar and 2 glasses of Montbazillac or Rosé de Provence.

Les Miques Frites
(Fried miques)

Time: 1 hour if you are making the miques; 10 minutes if they are already cooked.
Serves 4–6

3 Miques (see p. 26)   Castor sugar, redcurrant jelly or
Walnut or olive oil   honey for garnish
2 eggs, beaten

When the Miques are cold, slice them to form rounds about ½ inch (1.2 cm) thick. Dip the slices into beaten eggs and fry in hot oil. Serve on a heated dish dusted with castor sugar or garnished with redcurrant jelly or honey.

NOTES ON WINE TERMS

Throughout this book certain French words have been used because they describe a particular culinary process more succinctly than could be done in English. Viticulture and vinification are two such subjects, where a single French word expresses to perfection a particular object, condition or process and I have therefore adopted French terms where there is no English succinct equivalent. The terms most commonly on the tongue are:

VENDANGE:	The grape harvest.
VIGNOBLE(S):	Vineyard(s) planted with superior grape-types producing fine wine that conforms to strictly defined standards.
CÉPAGE(S):	Vine plant species.
CRU(S):	The vintage. Wine produced from a vineyard's best placed vines is referred to as the vineyard's 'Premier Cru'.

Few people (other than Frenchmen) are aware of the work that goes into producing a fine wine. Fine wine is not 'a happy accident'. The fermented juice of grapes can become 'a little miracle' but to the men devoted to the development of the miracle, joining and warring with the elements, there is nothing rarefied about their occupation. The serendipity of mineral, vegetable and climate must be bonded with ingenuity and incessant, impassioned travail, by experimentation with cépages, by matching cépage to situation, by the development of pest resistance. Viticulture, like agriculture and horticulture, is a Risk Business – and the vignobles of Périgord have been the victims of one of the business' 'unhappy accidents'.

THE WINES OF PÉRIGORD

The phylloxera is a species of louse particularly given to attacking vines. Between 1877 and 1883 the finest crus of Périgord were decimated by this pest – a loss of some 132 square kilometres of vines. The best wines of Domme, St Cyprien, St Pantelys, Beyzonac and St Vincent were given their death-blow. Apart from the vignobles of Bergerac, what vignobles survived the phylloxera were finally put out of business by the prohibitive taxes imposed on the Périgord wine-growers by their competitors fortunate enough to be further downstream than themselves. The Dordogne, the Isle and the Vézère carried the barges laden with casks of Périgord wine to the ports of Bergerac and Libourne and the drop in Périgordin production could not support the high duty demanded by these ports.

For the moment, then, the wines of Bergerac are all that remains of the fine wines of Périgord. The restitution of a vineyard is a slow and costly business. The fight to beat drought and pest has resulted in a system of cultivation by grafting. Certain wild vines are resistant to phylloxera, for instance, but the wine they produce is mediocre. The root is therefore used as stock (or porte-gréffe) for a species producing a better quality wine. Much of the Bergerac wine comes from cépages grafted onto American stock and there are growers in some of the erstwhile vignobles districts who hope to revive the wines of Périgord by such methods of cultivation.

The Wines of Bergerac

Bergerac lies on the river Dordogne towards its western reaches. The slopes rising from the right bank are a natural continuation of the slopes of St Emilion and Castillon and those rising from the left bank a continuation of the Entre Deux Mers. By its cultivation and soil the landscape seems closer to the Gironde than to the Department, the Dordogne and Périgord.

The left bank is the birthplace of the *Montbazillac* of which Alexandre Dumas said one should go down on one's knees and thank God as the wine touches the lips. It is a rich, sweet white wine grown only within the communes of Montbazillac, Pomport, Colombier, Rouffignac and parts of Saint-Laurent-des-Vignes. Fine wines are all a blend of cépages and Montbazillac is no exception, being the product of three cépages – the Sémillon-blanc, the Muscadelle and the Sauvignan – the same cépages as the Sauternes, but in different proportions. The fruit of these three plants grown in that particular soil combine to give the Montbazillac its unique flavour, aroma and colour, but the secret of the wine lies in knowing when to gather the three grape-types, in gauging exactly the moment when the level of sugar in each is '*à point*'. (This is, of course, the case for all fine wines – all *wine*, in fact – some of which may be a blend of four or more cépages, none of which may reach perfection at the best moment for the rest. Did I not say it was the Risk Business?)

Other white wines are those of *Côtes de Montravel* and *Haut-Montravel*, the produce of the cépages – the Enrageat and the blanc de Gaillac – within the limits of the canton of Vélines and the communes of Montpeyroux and Saint-Méard-de-Gurçon in the canton of Villfranche-de-Lonchard. There is also a dry white wine from Montravel, made predominantly from the Sauvignan.

The *Rosette*, which is grown to the north of Bergerac, is a fresh, agreeable semi-sweet wine of a rather unusual yellow colour. The Bergerac red wines issue from the Malbec, Cabernet, Merlot, Fer and Périgord cépages. They usually reach 10° or 11° but in certain years go as high as 12°. There are the red 'appellation controlée' wines:

LE BERGERAC: A fruity wine of a good ruby colour.
LES CÔTES DE
  BERGERAC: A darker, fruitier wine with a very good aroma.
LE PÊCHARMANT: The most illustrious of all the Bergerac reds. A wine that keeps well.

OTHER WINES

The Bergerac wines are all that is left of the Grands Crus de Périgord, but they aren't the only wines produced in the region. There are *hundreds* of vineyards in Périgord, as many, almost, as there are vegetable gardens. Nearly every household in this commune owns a vineyard – but the wine is for home consumption only.

At one time the vines planted in these vineyards would have been the Noah, the Otello, the Jaquas, the Clinton, the Herbemont – some of which (particularly the Noah) are said to contain a drug that may drive a man insane and it is now against the law to plant these vines. The hybrid vines now planted in local vineyards have nothing but an official number to distinguish them – so much that was homely or charming has been put to flight by officialdom. Where are the cows called Blossom and Daisy? They are number 96 and 97. In general, only two cépages are planted domestically and each man follows his own convictions on vinification. Mme Robert's husband, for instance, (who has 500 *'pieds'*) leaves his wine in the vat longer than anyone else, whereas old Mme Tuyot's son bottles his fairly quickly. A stranger walking through the village at this season would be surprised to see a litre bottle of wine on every doorstep – it is the custom to give every household a bottle of the new wine. The vendange is a communal affair and when the grapes are '*à point*' a rota is drawn up to decide the order of the harvest; it is All Hands to the Grape and as each crop is brought in All Hands are given a good meal by the owner of each vineyard. The wine is for daily consumption and doesn't keep long. M. Tonneau (who doesn't have a vineyard) estimates the *average* daily dose per household to be 1½ litres – the *exceptions* are the 6–11 litres a day men (one of whom describes sleeping off his intake as 'allowing his wine to ferment in his vat').

SUGGESTIONS ON THE SERVING OF WINE

My remarks on viticulture and vinification apply to the wines of south-west France. They may also apply to the wines of other regions such as the Burgundies, the Alsaces and the Champagnes but it is the clarets and whites of the south-west that concern me. In general the food and the wine of the region go well together and the following suggestions relate to these wines only.

The important word in the heading of this section is 'suggestion'; it is impossible to give the definitive wine for a dish, ridiculous to say that such-and-such a wine *must* be drunk with such-and-such a recipe. The best one can do is to name those wines that, either through personal experience or the experience of experts, have proved to have balanced and brought out the best in the food and the wine itself. This is a book on the Périgord, but as I have explained in this chapter, the only wines of 'premier cru' in the region are those of Bergerac and it would be foolish to limit oneself to the wines of that relatively small area when there is the whole of the Bordelais at one's disposal. The Périgordins drink a great deal of Bordeaux – I have only once been offered a Burgundy in the 10 years of my life here and that was by a Frenchman who was not from Périgord.

Until recent years, most English people did not understand the place of wine in a meal. Wine is not merely a pleasant way of taking in alcohol; it is an enrichment, an enhancement of a particular dish, a two way enhancement and enrichment, for the dish itself may bring out subtleties in the wine that might be missed were it taken alone. An appreciation and understanding of wine and its proper use has been developed by the superb marketing and presentation of wines in certain food chain-stores throughout Great Britain and though it might be thought that the explanatory labels along the wine racks could start an epidemic of wine snobbery, they have to my mind given wine the dignity of its natural and proper place.

Soups
(Particularly if you are going to do *Le Chabrol*).
Wine suggestion (reds): Bergerac, Bordeaux Côtes de Blaye or Côtes de Castillon.

Omelettes
Important principle – *never* white wine with eggs.
A simple omelette:

Wine suggestion: Pécharmant, Graves, Cahors.
An omelette with cèpes or truffles:
    Wine suggestion: St Emilion, Médoc

Foie gras
Served cold (i.e. pâté or terrine).
Wine suggestion: It is the fashion these days to drink sweet white wine with pâté, such as Montbazillac or Sauterne.

Served hot (i.e. Stuffed Tomatoes or *en feuillté):*
Wine suggestion: The very best Bordeau Rouge you can afford.

Fish, Shell-fish, etc.
Wine suggestion: Entre-Deux-Mers, Graves Sec.

Meat
Wine suggestion: The best 'Reds' of Bergerac and Bordeaux (Mouton-Rothschild, Pomerol, St Emilion, Margaux etc.)

Poultry, Poultry with Truffles
Wine suggestion: Graves Rouge, Pauillac, Côtes de Castillon.

Game
Wine suggestion: St Emilion, Pomerol, a good Médoc.

Sauces
Note: It is a mistake to use an inferior wine in a sauce.
Sauce made with white wine: Barsac, Graves, Sauternes.

Sauce made with red wine: A good Bergerac, Cahors

Vegetables and Stews
Wine suggestion: Pécharmant, St Emilion, Cahors.

Mushrooms and Cèpes
Wine suggestion: St Emilion, Margaux

Truffles
Wine suggestion: Pomerol, Médoc, Pauillac.

Salads
Opinions are divided here. Some say 'Just fresh water'; others continue to drink the wine served at the meat course.

Walnuts and Cheese

Here again opinions differ, some preferring white wine with their walnuts and cheese. I myself follow the example of the Head Steward on an Air France flight who opened a good red Bordeaux for me to drink with my tiny triangle of Camembert. (I understood why when my Carte Bleu statement came through ... I thought it was wonderful service for Economy Class.)

Sweets

Wine suggestion: *Montbazillac, of course!*

Ices and Sorbets

Wine suggestion: Sorbet 'specialists' drink water with this dessert. I suggest Champagne – my only concession to the other regions of France.

With your coffee

In your coffee: A good eau-de-vie de Périgord.

LES LIQUEURS
(APÉRITIFS AND DIGESTIFS)

Nature and Man are inseparable and nowhere is this more apparent than in Périgord. The beauty and richness of Périgord have infiltrated the bloodstream of its men and women, heightening their senses and awareness to a remarkable degree, and their use of leaves in the making of apéritifs is a perfect example of their rapport with their surroundings. Infusions made from the leaves of lime trees and various herbs are quite common throughout the world, as is the use of certain shrubs for flavouring dishes, but the fact that the leaves of fruit trees impregnate alcohol with the scent and flavour of the fruit they bear is not well-known. In Périgord extremely good apéritifs and digestifs are made in every home and the following selection can be made without difficulty outside the region. With the exception of the Eau-de-Coing (Quince liqueur), all these recipes came from our greatest local exponent of the art, and though I have tasted many excellent drinks in other houses I have chosen these recipes because they seem to me to have the most refinement – perhaps because they contain less sugar than those of other people.

I must point out that not all fruit-tree leaves are usable for flavouring drinks. Redcurrant leaves, for instance, are not a success, and the only cherry leaf with sufficient 'parfum' is that of the morello.

Important notes:

1 The alcohol used in making these drinks should have *no flavour of its own*. Pure alcohol can be bought at the chemist in France. Failing that, use vodka, though its alcohol content is slightly lower.
2 It is essential to use new, clean corks, or screw-top bottles.

L'Apéritif d'Orange
(Orange aperitif)

The skin of 5 oranges (they need not be peeled especially, simply keep the skins when you press or eat an orange)
1 clove

1 pt (575 ml) alcohol at 45°–60°
4 pts (2 l) sweet white wine
12 oz (375 g) castor sugar, or less, according to taste

Put the orange skins, the clove and the alcohol into a kilner jar. Close hermetically and leave for 3 weeks. Poke the skins with the handle of a wooden spoon occasionally during the 3 weeks to impregnate the alcohol with their flavour.

Boil the wine and the sugar for 5 minutes. Strain the liquid from the kilner jar into the wine and sugar, stir gently to mix them and bottle. Keep a year before using.

Le Vin d'Orange
(Orange wine)

3 bitter oranges
8 oz (250 g) of sugar
1 glass of eau-de-vie or Cognac

2 pt (1 l) of white wine
1 tbsp of chicory powder or liquid.

Peel 3 bitter oranges thinly, avoiding the pith. (Spanish oranges with the 'untreated' guarantee are the best.) Dissolve the sugar in a little heated white wine and put it into a kilner jar with the orange peel, the chicory powder/liquid and the eau-de-vie or Cognac. Add a bottle of dry white wine. Close hermetically and leave for a week. Strain and bottle.

L'Apéritif aux Feuilles de Cassis
(Blackcurrant aperitif)

50 blackcurrant leaves
8 oz (250 g) of sugar

1 wineglass of Kirsch
2 pt (1 l) dry white wine

Put 50 blackcurrant leaves into a kilner jar and pour in a glass of

Kirsch. Dissolve the sugar in 1 litre of dry white wine and add it to the kilner jar. Make airtight and leave it for a week. Strain and bottle.

Le Vin de Pêche
(Peach wine)

For 6 pints (2.5 l) of wine:

4 pt (2 l) of white wine
8 oz (250 g) of castor sugar
2 cloves
5 or 6 peach kernels

6 large yellow peaches
1 vanilla pod
½ pt (300 ml) of eau-de-vie

Peel the peaches, leave them whole and put them into a large kilner jar. Add the kernels, the vanilla pod and the cloves. Pour the white wine over the peaches, seal the jars hermetically and leave in a cool place (not the refrigerator) for 1 week. At the end of the week, strain the liquid through a fine cloth, add the sugar and the eau-de-vie and bottle. Serve chilled.

Note: The peaches make a delicious pudding sprinkled with chopped walnuts or cooked and served as a compôte.

Le Digestif de Genièvre
(Juniper digestif)

2 pt (1 l) of eau-de-vie or similar
   alcohol
2 oz (50 g) of green juniper
   berries

8 oz (250 g) of castor sugar
2 oz (50 g) black juniper berries
½ pt (300 ml) of water
The grated peel of 1 orange

Melt the sugar in the water. Put all the ingredients into a 4-pint (2-litre) kilner jar, make it airtight and leave to steep for 3 weeks in a cool place (not the refrigerator). Strain through a fine cloth, bottle and allow to mature for a year or so.

L'Apéritif aux Feuilles de Pêche
(Peach leaf aperitif)

120 peach leaves
1 bottle of Rosé de Provence

25 lumps of sugar
1 glass of Kirsch

Collect 120 peach leaves between 15 August and 15 September. Wash them and dry them in a clean cloth. Put them into a jar with the Rosé de Provence, the sugar and the Kirsch, make airtight and leave for 5 days. After 5 days strain and bottle.

L'Apéritif aux Feuilles de Noix
(Walnut leaf aperitif)

Handfuls of walnut leaves
   (2 good handfuls to
   every 2 pt (1 l) alcohol)
	Red wine
	2 pt (1 l) of alcohol (60°)
	Sugar

Gather handfuls of walnut leaves whilst they are still of reddish tinge (about 15 July). Leave them to soak in the alcohol for 3 weeks. Stir occasionally. After 3 weeks strain. Take one glass of the liquid obtained and add to a bottle of goodish red wine, continuing thus until the liquid from the leaves is used up. Measure the total amount of liquid. Dissolve 4 oz (125 g) of sugar for every litre of wine obtained in a little heated wine. Add the melted sugar to the mixture of alcohol and wine and bottle.

Le Digestif de L'Eau de Vie de Coing
(Quince liqueur)

For every 25 lb (10 kg) of quinces allow 2 pt (1 l) of alcohol (60°) and 2½ lb (1 kg) of sugar

Peel the fruit and grate them. Squeeze the grated flesh to extract all the juice. Pour the juice into a crock with the sugar and leave it to settle for 24 hours. Measure the liquid and for every 6 pints (3 litres) of juice add 2 pints (1 litre) of alcohol (60°). Leave for 15 days. At the end of this time filter and bottle. Store on their sides in a moderate temperature. Leave one year before using. This wine improves in quality and 'parfum' with age.

La Confiture Vieux Garçons
(Old Boys' Liqueur)

This is a powerful concoction of alcohol and every fruit available throughout the seasons.

As each fruit comes into season put a layer into a large jar with a covering of sugar and just enough alcohol at 60° to keep the fruit covered. Continue adding layers of fruit, sugar and alcohol (say, raspberries, strawberries, cherries, redcurrants, nectarines, blackberries, sliced banana, etc., etc.) until the jar is full. Keep hermetically closed throughout. If *possible*, keep at least a year. Serve at the end of a meal with the coffee, in little liqueur glasses and a spoon, just a few

bits of fruit and a little covering of the liquid. Leave the stalks on the cherries so that one can pick them out easily without using a spoon. The only fruits not really suitable are the hard fruits of autumn.

This is another aspect of HEAVEN and must resign, if not actually send, the vieux garçons to it.

Le Canard

When you come to the fruit course, cut an apple in slices, dip each slice in sugar and then in eau-de-vie-de prune (or the liqueur available to you).

An orange is also eaten in this manner, always at the coffee and liqueur stage of a meal, and this is called *Le Canard*.

Glossary

al dente	(Ital: to the tooth) cooked until still firm when bitten.
à point	Cul: cooked to perfection. Of fruit: exactly ready for picking.
Baking blind	Pastry cooked empty, to be filled later.
Blanch	Immerse in boiling water.
Bouillon	Stock or gruel.
Caul	The French word 'Crépine' is translated by 'Caul' in the dictionaries, but 'Crépine' is in fact a fine membrane lining the belly of sheep and pigs. The dictionary has been used here because no specific equivalent terms has been found.
Civet	Jugged, or stewed in wine.
Court bouillon	Stock made from wine, vegetables and herbs, usually for cooking fish.
Crotted	Fouled, soiled. ('Crottes de poule': hen droppings.)
Doré	Fry until soft and golden, but not completely cooked.
Flambé	Alcohol set alight.
Fricassée	Raw or cooked vegetables, lightly fried.
Hachis	Herbs, garlic or onion chopped together and used as a garnish or to flavour a dish.
Lardons	Lardings or small pieces of streaky bacon or breast of pork.
Nappe	Coat with a sauce.
Pied(s)	Foot(Feet). Bot: Cutting, or root of a plant. (A vineyard of 5,000 pieds = 500 vines).
Ragoût	Stew. In Périgord a 'ragout' is the name given to cooking certain vegetables (See Section).
Salmi	A stew or casserole of partly roasted game birds, finished in a wine stock.
Sobriquet	Nick-name.

Toupine	Earthenware or Terracotta interior-glazed pot for storing pâtés, conserves, fat etc.
Traiteur	Chef or caterer.
Vedette	A Star (Theatrical).
Verjuice	Liquid pressed from unripe grapes or crab apples.

INDEX